THINKING WITH THE EYE'S MIND

THINKING WITH THE EYE'S MIND

Dynamic Planning in a Time of Chaos and Disruption

David Herman

Published by Scotia Place Publishing

www.u-template.com

Contact author at davidherman@vodafone.co.nz

A catalogue record for this book is available from the National Library of New Zealand.

Sketches by Lawrence Buck.

Much thanks to Jay Bitsack at Acore ll for your invaluable input and expertise.

CONTENTS

TESTIMONIALS

"... an intellectual tour de force."
—*Judy Schramm, Director, ProResource*

"This is **exactly** what Dr Tom English of the US Navy's weapons safety board was talking about when he said he wanted to see integrated analyses (plural), rather than separate analyses stapled together with a cover sheet. Zounds my man, you've got a breakthrough!!"
—*Mathew Weilert, Director, The Systems Thinking Institute"*

"Clearly the structuring of thoughts, knowledge and human interaction into a process and cogent organization is a challenge that is quite ubiquitous. I think your Ford example (on the U-Template) does a great job of highlighting both the problem and solution."
—*Michael Loria, Vice President, Corporate and Business Development IBM Security and Mobile. Formerly IBM Business Development Rational Software*

"This is much more than a project tool. The ability to track the spectrum of information from the data requirements makes it one of the best tools I have seen."
—*Cameron Erikson, MVP Healthcare*

"I'm impressed with your work and believe it carries significant potential to stimulate interest in the U-Template and the related 10 Pillars...I find valuable insight in the

connections you've made between improving human cognition and the use of visual/graphic imagery."
—*Jay Bitsack, Practice Director, ACORE II (Bus, Tech & TLS Transformation Services)*

EXCERPTS

From *Thinking With the Eye's Mind*

To be more specific, innovative thinking and planning—and by "planning" I'm referring to any future-oriented thought process—often entails a certain amount of
mental preparation, (more-or-less unconscious), in which
we first tentatively survey the task at hand and in doing
so, lay the groundwork for a more intensive identification
of both the problems that lie before us and the actions we
might take to alleviate them. As part of this process, perhaps the most essential part, we initially herd the ideas we
already have in mind into a kind of mental holding pen,
the conceptual space in which they—and others that might
follow—will be sorted out and consolidated into a suitable
plan of action.

At any rate, this advanced level of self-orientation, this firm
grasp of both our immediate and up-and-coming circumstances known as "situation awareness" exemplifies the
kind of comprehensive perthinking that allows us to see
through the surface of things, through financial markets
and battlefields, deep down to their profoundest indications for the immediate and long-term future. At bottom,
it's the exceptional knack for incorporating facts on the
ground (including the other guy's perception of that same
ground) into a deep and farsighted perspective. It's about
staying on top of things, so that nothing untoward is likely

to happen that we hadn't already prepared for at least twice over.

This notion of emergence might very well apply to the "system" you yourself might be constructing at this very moment, let's say ... a new and novel project-worthy idea (and yes, ideas that "accept input and provide output" can be thought of as systems). Indeed, this brainstorm of yours might have occurred to you just recently and so, still in its embryonic stage, it lies there partially out of sight and mind, waiting to emerge at the first opportunity, lights flashing and bells ringing.

AUTHOR'S NOTE

PUTTING THINGS IN PERSPECTIVE

As I set out to write this book, my purpose was to introduce the U-Template ("Universal Template") as an aid to planning and developing new and innovative ideas with the help of a few accompanying observations as to the benefits of non-linear project analysis. But by the time I had finished compiling my notes I realized that the material I had intended to explore amounted to just one part of a larger and more fundamental equation: namely how our perspective widens—and hence our foresight—when we think with our "eye's mind".

To be more specific, innovative thinking and planning—and by "planning" I'm referring to any future-oriented thought process—often entails a certain amount of mental preparation, (more-or-less unconscious), in which we first tentatively survey the task at hand and in doing so, lay the groundwork for a more intensive identification of both the problems that lie before us and the actions we might take to alleviate them. As part of this process, perhaps the most essential part, we initially herd the ideas we already have in mind into a kind of mental holding pen, the conceptual space in which they—and others that might follow—will be sorted out and consolidated into a suitable plan of action.

This mental stocktaking procedure tends to work well

enough under ordinary circumstances: when the problems we face are run of the mill and most familiar to us. These we can often solve in our sleep, as the saying goes. That is, they can be treated (if it's at all possible) according to the established rules (of one rulebook or another), and once they're solved, they stay solved (e.g., math and grammatical problems are "tame" in such a way.) Such were the prevailing problems of pre-industrial societies, simple contingencies of primitive conditions. If you were a 17th century peasant, your problems (e.g., not enough rain, or no beer in the larder) might have been truly formidable but nevertheless reasonably tame. In other words, no problem was so complex that you couldn't find a workable solution—if there was one—using just a dash of know-how and common sense. This was also a time when problems were often easy enough to solve collectively, i.e. their apparent solutions could be readily articulated and communicated to others. In those agrarian days, people that worked together probably spoke the same language—both literally and figuratively—and shared similar perspectives on problem-solving methods and objectives. The standard treatment formula, at its best, remained the same, viz. follow an orderly and linear path: define the problem, decide what is to be done, and, finally, determine the performance standards necessary to get the job done properly.

But thinking and problem-solving with the help of relatively simple preparatory measures often comes to naught when the matters to be addressed are too fleeting, complex or ambiguous to size up in a single take, especially when the project's operational setting—namely the environment in which the plan is to be executed—is too volatile and transitory to indicate what "the playing field" will be like at the time the plan is to be put into operation.

Consequently, it's becoming more and more difficult to find our critical points of reference "out there", (outside of the relatively small systems in which we operate on a daily basis). As a consequence, the tenuousness and uncertainty of this first part of the 21st century is getting the better of us, reducing our "grounded-ness" and "situation awareness" to the point where we are all of us virtual strangers in a strange land, increasingly unsure of who we are, where we are, and where—we think—we're going.

One might say that today's problems are like untamed jungles: there are few signposts, they pose significant threats, and when you find yourself entangled in them they can scare the bejesus out of you[1]. They're plain wicked.

A "wicked problem" (as identified by design theorist Horst Rittel) has been described as a "class of social system problems which are ill-formulated, where the information is confusing, where there are many clients and decision makers with conflicting values, and where the ramifications in the whole system are thoroughly confusing." As you might imagine, problems of this nature rarely respond to standardized treatments, as few wicked problems are likely to be fundamentally alike. Lastly, due to their messy attributes, wicked problems have no right answers, only solutions that are "good enough".

So, as you're probably wondering, how do we deal with

---

1. Imagine that you've just been dropped into a densely tangled and uncharted jungle, fearing for your survival and without the least notion of how to get back to the safety of civilization. What's more, suppose that your means of survival in this case depends only on a single tool of our own choosing, only one and no more. Now, if you'd care to think about it, what in the world might that single item turn out to be? Could it be a compass, or possibly a device with a GPS unit, map, and compass combined given today's technology rich environment? And could such a guidance system, when linked to the right coordinates, afford us a decent read on our position, heading, and rate of progress? That's the U-Template.

today's inescapable mind-bogglers? Well, there are many options open to us, but as this book will show, there is one available course of action that is both readily do-able and immensely effective: the creation of an information-gathering "holding pen" combined with a personal or group planning mechanism that sets our bearings locally and largely in terms of our own personal sweep of vision.

(Which happens to be a most practical way to go about things—for we are all instinctive browsers, "looking machines", hardwired to forage throughout our immediate surroundings for recognizable objects that we might exploit for our immediate purposes. From early infancy we are busy looking around and gathering a "visual knowledge" our environment.)

David Herman

Auckland, April 2018

HOW TO USE THIS BOOK

Thinking with the Eye's Mind is divided into four parts with 14 chapters in all.

In addition to the book, there is a **free online application** that you can access from the book's website at **u-template.com**.

Part One

The first part introduces some of the key concepts and issues associated with thinking and ideas.

Chapter 1 points to several problems associated with so-called "reasoned" thinking and questions whether or not the brain might be designed biologically to approach its problem-solving tasks in a somewhat different manner.

Chapter 2 looks at an effective alternative to "pure reason": namely the holistic, non-linear, (evidence-based) perceptual thinking—or "perthinking"—of the eye's mind.

Chapter 3 adds recursive thinking (thinking-about-our-own-thinking) to the list of invaluable holistic, non-linear thinking techniques. We also consider scientist Gregory Bateson's surprising suggestion that a certain measure of uncertainty—regarding one's knowledge base—can be good for our investigative thinking.

Chapter 4 describes a certain keenly attuned state of mind known as "situation awareness", awareness as pattern recognition and how "idea structures" as meaningful patterns (of information) can be represented pictorially with the use of graphic organizers.

Chapter 5 describes a specific graphic organizer, the U-Template as "idea-sandwich", (its components piled one on top of another and sandwiched between ten specific judgement criteria for assessing one or more facets of the idea).

Part Two

Chapters 6 through 8 take a closer look at the U-Template and provides a set of instructions and tips for getting the most out of its visual-thinking approach. They also provide links to a demonstration website where you can observe the system in action and try it yourself.

Part Three

The third part now surveys the unconscious cerebral mechanisms that support both individual and group planning.

Chapter 9 opens with a few generalized thoughts concerning today's societal complexities and how we often fall back on intuition in our effort to struggle through them. Chess and chess masters are used as prime examples.

Chapter 10 takes an abrupt turn and examines personal (life-change) planning from the perspective of the mind's diverse and wide-ranging unconscious processes.

Chapter 11 puts the emphasis on the mental mechanics we know as goal-setting and explains how this behavior, both conscious and not-at-all-conscious, applies to personal life-change planning.

Part Four

Part Four offers a miscellany of commentary and information.

Chapter 12 is principally a synopsis of the systems-specific principles underlying the U-Template's non-linear, part-to-part/part-to-whole analysis.

Chapter 13 contains a few meditations on personal uncertainty, one of the project-related human factors monitored in the course of any U-Template project review.

Chapter 14 presents the U-Template's business rationale and is strictly for business owners and project managers.

INTRODUCTION

NEW IDEAS AND THE TRANSFORMATION OF REALITY

There are those that say that ideas are a dime a dozen. Well, I'm not so sure about the old adage, especially if it's supposed to include the kind of ideas that flower into projects designed to make the world a better place. However, even a promising idea can harbor problematic subordinate elements, major issues weighty enough to sink any program it might set in motion. Should this prove to be the case, the wannabe bright idea might not be worth a h**l of a lot, certainly not worth the time and effort it might take to develop it—warts and all—into a successful project. In fact, as it happens with many Hollywood "properties-in-development", a work in progress might require more time and energy spent on post- production adjustment than the resources spent getting it off the ground in the first place.

Now let me put this to you again, this time in the negative and in the form of two questions:

- Were you ever struck with what seemed at the time to be a terrific idea, so impressive at first glance that you decided that it just had to be too good to be true and that if it excited you so much there must be something wrong with it somewhere? So better forget the whole thing before it falls flat on its face and takes you with it.

- Or—have you ever abandoned a promising idea-cum-project on more sensible grounds, namely, for want of a trustworthy pre-production assessment procedure? This would be entirely understandable. So many decision-support tools are based on statistical concepts and methods well beyond our ken, so abstruse that they normally require the assistance of a paid consultant to translate their procedures and outcomes into plain language.

In either of these two scenarios, you may have finally scuttled the idea only to discover later on, when someone else ran with the idea, that you'd missed out on a good thing.

Well you needn't let this happen to you again. Not if you're willing to do a little homework and dare to be your own consultant. This book will show you, chapter-by-chapter, that there is no excuse for abandoning an idea that shows even a modicum of promise. There's no reason not to size up the idea yourself and, depending on what you find, either work it out to its conclusion as-is, try to rectify it, or, if there doesn't seem to be any other choice, yes, let it go. However, and here's the big "but", what you must do, and do before anything else, is get to the crux of your idea so that you can truly feel its beating heart and see what makes it tick.

Of course, conducting an in-depth analysis objectively is by no means an easy job. The human mind is simply not equipped to do this sort of thing coolly and without prejudice as, in all likelihood, early in our primate history, maintaining objectivity was not at all conducive to physical survival. To be dispassionate was to be disinterested, and to be disinterested was to be inattentive and disregardful of the world (read: jungle) all around us. But ever since, as objectivity is no longer a handicap, we've been developing helpful mediating devices to keep us at a proper distance from serious harm, such as electronic decision-support systems, the Universal Template (U-Template) for instance, a planning tool that plays to the strengths of our most discriminating cerebral mechanism, the "eye's mind" (not to be confused with the "mind's eye", it's not the same thing. Not at all the same.) Parenthetically, one often thinks of perception as a low-level activity whose sole task is to supply the thinking part of the brain with raw material, during which time our perceptions are translated, edited, and made "sensible", i.e. first you see it then you think about it. But psychologists now tend to believe that perception and cognition are highly intertwined and that to a greater extent than one might imagine, perception *is* cognition. And, as you'll soon observe, much of what we refer to as thinking is more often than not a largely visio-spatial recognition process (which I'll refer to from here on in as "perthinking").

The Universal Template, the thinking and planning device (and the core subject of this book), represents a radical departure from your standard decision-support approach, e.g., the formulaic/algorithmic quantifications that consultants are known to foist on the unwary. Rather than reduce investigative outcomes to bare numbers, the U-Template "perspectivizes" ideas, revealing the strengths and weaknesses of developmental projects with the help of common words and phrases arranged so as to provide clues to the project's likely viability.

In the following chapters, you'll be introduced to an idea-testing and project-planning method that you can use to map out business or life-changing strategies with a new sense of confidence in your own personal powers of judgement, a method that will provide you with the self-assurance you'll need when it's time to take one last look at your latest idea and answer the proverbial question: "Do I do it, or do I drop it?" So please read this book carefully and with your imagination wide open to a new cognitive/perceptual experience. I promise you that after giving the U-Template a few trial runs, you'll never walk away from a worthwhile idea again.

If you have doubts in this regard, let me assure you that the notion of perceptual "bootstrapping" isn't as far-fetched as it might seem. In fact, most of it occurs unconsciously, as part of our natural biological development. As the human brain adapts to the natural and man-made aspects of the world through experience, it becomes more adroit at making fine distinctions; that is, it learns to discriminate between different classes of object categories (e.g., between automobiles by differentiating between a Ford and Toyota, or between two musical notes on a scale by distinguishing between an e and an e-flat). Paradoxically, we also tend to become less sensitive to the differences between two instances of the same object category (e.g., we learn to stay clear of all large cats, from the mountain lynx to the Bengal tiger). All in all, each time we go out of our way to separate things through differentiations or combine things through broad generalizations, we sharpen our ability to recognize patterns of sensory data that have the power to alert us to looming threats or opportunities. This is true of any "perthought", we're likely to have in such circumstances, ranging from our reactions to the simplest sensory input (e.g., a loud crash) to our more integrated responses to visual spatial and temporal patterns, such as the rapidly shifting strategies of a champion chess match.

Oh, and by the way, while this book touches on many of the creative aspects of visual-thinking, it's not about creativity per se, nor is it about the art of generating creative ideas. You can find this sort of advice in the countless books that already fill the shelves of your neighborhood bookstore. *Thinking with the Eye's Mind* picks up where these other books leave off: helping you decide whether or not your recent "brainchild" as you've conceived it so far, is a good-enough child to raise to adulthood within the framework of a serious and time-consuming project. Having said this, I will add that this book does indeed talk about creative ideas as they apply specifically to visual imagery, holistic thinking, human intuition, and all the other mental processes you'll bring to bear on a bright idea the next time one of these potential goldmines just happens to pop into your head.

In closing, I can't guarantee that you'll be as excited as I am by the factual and theoretical matters discussed in the upcoming chapters, but I can tell you without hesitation that as a practical guide to making better plans, this book...well...it delivers. So, if you're willing to work your way through the following pages assiduously and with an open mind, I'm certain that you'll soon find what you would hope to find, something you can actually use—the U-Template, a simple instrument for making complex plans along with a planning method as simple and practical as a cast-iron skillet.

PART I

KEY CONCEPTS FOR BUSINESS AND INSTITUTIONAL PLANNING

CHAPTER 1

WHERE ORDINARY
PROBLEM-SOLVING FAILS US

The deliberate process we call reasoning is, I believe, the thinnest veneer of human thought, effective only because it is supported by this much older and much more powerful, though usually unconscious, sensorimotor knowledge.
— *John Dewey*

… our ideas are often subverted by the long chains of associated mental material that rattle along behind them.

The biggest question driving our unrelentingly uphill struggles to plan ahead in an age of pervasive uncertainty may very well be this: how do we manage to survive a 21st century day with only a limited repertoire of rather fallible mental processes to guide our efforts? We don't always think satisfactorily in the best of situations, so how do we actually manage to meet the strict and ever-changing imperatives of our chaotic post-modern world? How do we ever manage to think our way to our—surprisingly numerous—happy endings?

Believe it or not, after decades of research it's still hard to say. Our well-grounded descriptions of the human cognitive process, such as they are, tell us little about the intrinsic nature of our day-to-day reasoning activities.[1] All we know for sure is that the human animal makes regular use of some sort of quasi-logical problem-solving procedure that frequently proves to be fairly well focused and ultimately goal directed. Which is to say that despite the wide-ranging dissimilarities of our personal thinking styles, we all tend to base our reasoning on specific propositions that we believe to be true (e.g., all cats are animals), apply them to the instances we have in mind (e.g., Felix is a cat), and finally arrive at conclusions that are most likely to be valid under these terms (therefore, Felix is an animal).

But is this 99.5% all-thinking process sure to get us to where we want to go? Case in point: based on the (tacit) proposition that runs something like, "Thinking is the province of sentient beings that do in fact exist", René Descartes, the "I"-that-thinks, leaped confidently to his seemingly airtight conclusion, "Therefore, I am." But

---

1. Human reasoning rarely depends on pure reason". It relies instead on some sort of personal or communal "mental maps" with which we chart our everyday activities.

sorry, Descartes, your homespun logic won't get us very far. Not by a mile, according to your innumerable critics. The "I think therefore I am" bit ... well, you can drive a truck through the holes of the argument from start to finish. So maybe our (verbal, non-mathematical) would-be logical thinking is not so very logical after all.[2]

Not only do we make questionable deductions more often than we'd prefer to, but as cognitive psychologists point out, we just as often fall victim to our own "indirect" reasoning: unconscious inferences based on flawed assumptions and/or mental models (e.g., " ... because only an x or a y person" we (prejudicially) assume "would do such a [wonderful, nasty, meaningless, etc.] thing, a worrying tendency when one considers it, inasmuch as these world views are often based on early, often traumatic and dissociated childhood experiences. Moreover, when called upon to consider relatively important matters, even the most diligent of us occasionally drift off-course into meandering reveries. Yes, these "streams of consciousness"[3] do keep us in touch with other, more personal, problems, (our unconscious mind is trying to work them out on its own terms), but they are the farthest thing imaginable from logical thinking.

But what is most worrying in these instances of mental discontinuity, is that we often fall victim to ill-founded reasoning processes precisely at those times when we are in the greatest need of truly rational and coherent deliberation. For example, when we're putting together broad

---

2. Purely rational thought, the experts tell us, is objective and free of any species of human emotion. (Yeah, right.)

3. One might think of these free-flowing meditations as mere wool-gathering, but take it from a one-time psychoanalyst: on some level and in one way or another, we're almost always trying to work out some nagging problem with sketchy impromptu scenarios in which we play out our greatest hopes or fears.

strategies or detailed plans on which our very survival may depend , our ideas are often subverted by the long chains of associated mental material that rattle along behind them. The influence of this extra psychic load will hinge on, first, its age and current condition and second, its degree of correspondence with those "background" thoughts to which it is somehow attached. Of course, due to reality's infinite variety and the memory's easy slippage, very few of these mental associations will interconnect point after point, and the rational correspondence between mentations will be even more dubious when there is no readily available match of any sort: in such cases, the psychic connection might instead be based loosely on a rough or fanciful analogy. Although in certain circumstances, chain-like thinking may be relatively efficient, or at least seem so at the time, its practicality and reliability will be limited by the narrowness of its bandwidth and the excessive influence of the most recent addition(s) to the chain.[4] In summary, there's a downside to virtually all domino-effect thought processes, often an inflexible backward determinism that, when in full force, makes it difficult for us to think "outside of the chain" and into the unfettered present.

Many of the troubles that afflict our more intricate mental processes are the product of mere human imperfection and the pernicious effect our thinking habits can have on our broad-based judgments. In business, the most learned and seasoned professionals, in-house or brought-in-from-elsewhere, will typically bring with them their own agendas, preferences, and biases, not to mention their social (teamwork) and analytic deficiencies. These

---

4. Over and above the pernicious influence of ideas that have been chained together every which way, these bits and pieces of older material—they are memories after all—are likely to be far too personal in an autobiographical sense to serve as the basis of dispassionate thinking.

shortcomings are known as cognitive biases and there are dozens of them.

EXAMPLES OF COGNITIVE BIASES

- The availability bias, which refers to the tendency to give additional weight to information that is relatively recent or prominent in one way or another.
- The anchoring bias, the tendency to rely too heavily on the first piece of information that comes along.
- The confirmation bias, the tendency to accept information that supports one's own opinions; and, of course, the Mother of all Biases.
- The "confidence" bias, which refers to our (and I do mean all of us) tendency to trust our own opinions without reservation, even in the face of strong evidence to the contrary or highly conflicting personal experience.

Of course, one must also be mindful of those hidden biases that spring from our very deepest unconscious processes. Did you ever have a passing thought that somehow disappeared into thin air, its absence entirely unnoticed until the very same idea, for no apparent reason, somehow slipped right back into its proper place? This wholesale disappearance of cognitive material might well have been the work of your mind's "coordinating editor". (One might also claim that this mental vanishing act is the work of the unconscious mental censor that Freud constantly cited, but I'm not going to get into that argument here.) This all-powerful Suppressor, whatever it may be, might have commandeered your thoughts for any number of conceivable reasons, not the least of which could be, as the psychologist Leon Festinger brings to our attention, the abandonment of (good) ideas that clash in a "dissonant" way with other (not-so-good) ideas. Being committed to them, we might effectually separate them conceptually through the imposition of makeshift or spurious differentiations (e.g., "It's OK, the grapes (I didn't get) were probably sour anyway.").[5]

So how familiar are you with the biases you carry around in your mind from day to day? How did they get there? How were they assimilated into your world view? Keep in mind that as with all of our mental habits, our personal biases tend to share the same characteristics, which is one reason we often respond to telling remarks made by familiar people with the classic rejoinder, "I knew you'd say that!"

---

5. The inclination to avoid legitimate self-doubt is characteristic of those we would least expect to be so afflicted: soldiers, lawyers, and psychologists, to name a few examples. Barry M. Straw describes one of the most potentially catastrophic of these tendencies as the "sunk cost" bias in his so very aptly titled "Knee Deep in the Big Muddy," in which he discusses the common tendency—so bone-headedly obtuse that it often ignites howls of derision when it reveals itself in (someone else's) behavior—to confirm the rightness of an earlier and wrong-headed behavior by stubbornly duplicating it no matter what the consequences. The old adages "in for a penny, in for a pound" or "good money after bad" summarize this tendency quite well.

CHAPTER 2

IF THE IDEA FITS, WEAR IT

$$R_{\mu\nu} - \frac{1}{2} R g_{\mu\nu} = \frac{8\pi G}{c^4} T_{\mu\nu}$$

We trust the "Aha!" feelings that come over us when we finally "see the whole picture".

There are many schools of thought that hold that human reasoning need not depend on ... well, reason (as-we-know-it), and that we tend to monitor our everyday activities with non-linear analytic methods based on personal or communal "mental maps". Such one-shot decision-making procedures (where the mind reasons things out in one fell swoop) can be effective across a wide range of speculative activities, the fuzzily intuitive and unformulated on one end of the spectrum, and the scrupulously analytical and well-structured on the other. Perhaps this principle of "best accordance" was best expressed by the psychologist William James when he said, "Truth is verifiable to the extent that thoughts and statements correspond with actual things, as well as 'hangs together,' or coheres, fits as pieces of a puzzle might fit together …" James's picture-puzzle-like validation process is also apparent in the tenets of coherentism, a school of thought that subscribes to the notion of truth based on the argumentative power of mutually-supporting pieces of evidence, the relational stuff that lies between the facts and binds them together. According to the latter, a set of beliefs about a circumstance or event that coheres internally—as well as with the apparent "facts"—ultimately provides its own legitimacy. Conversely, a set of faulty ideas displaying "self-revealing inconsistencies" will not. It will defeat itself the moment it's applied to things that "people know inside and out". (How this notion applies to political matters here in the second decade of the 21st century is another matter.)

According to many other philosophers and psychologists, a proposition is validated by the consonance and "fit" of the elements that together constitute its implicit scenario. Coherentism argues that you have a good reason to conclude that "the dog did it" if you also believe that the pieces of evidence that support this conclusion are "reasonable in light of one another". You see that your favorite pillow has been torn to pieces and that Rover, wearing his occasional "hangdog" look, is cowering in a corner covered head to tail with odd bits of assorted feathers.

While the coherentists ask why something is true, the abductionists, applying much the same criteria to "new and outside ideas," are more interested in how things come to pass. (The U-Template, which I'll describe at length before long, asks the same questions, but looks to the future as well as the past, demonstrating (or disconfirming) that "this is how it should happen in all probability".) And while coherentism is concerned with the structure and content of a given argument, abductive thinkers are more interested in the process by which the argument crystalized, preferring explanatory notions on the basis of the so-very-pragmatic "it's the best instance of what's worth considering".

Charles Sanders Peirce, who might rightly be described as the King of Common Sense, first used the term "abduction"—in reference to "induction" with "inference to the past"—as a form of educated supposition. And perhaps he was right to do so, insofar as that which we all hold to be true, (e.g., that the sun will rise if tomorrow is a cloudless day), is, at the end of the day, little more than (well-supported) guesswork.

Abduction allows for a precondition to be abduced from the vantage point of its ultimate consequence, and while it's a reasoning process that's clearly fallacious in a strict sense, it's not without a certain utility in its hum-drum day-to-day application. Overall, it's a pretty fair description of the manner in which we tend to cobble together our routine perceptions into rough conclusions. For example, when we see a bus rolling toward us, we may legitimately abduce that it started its journey with the help of the bus driver currently sitting behind the wheel. But there are many other possible explanations for this current state of affairs, such as "not long ago, the bus was parked on a steep hill (with the hand brake off) when a slight seismic tremor sent it merrily on its way". But why bother with this last hypothesis if, as we well know, the ground hasn't rumbled at all and the local landscape is perfectly flat?

I should add at this point that abductive thinking's inferential approach must have something going for it, as scientists, artificial intelligence experts, production-process executives, fault-diagnosis consultants, and software application engineers all make good use of it, trusting that the proof is in the pudding-mix, and that explanations built on credible patterns of information can be far more useful than those that lean heavily on deductive reasoning alone. For example, an explanation of inter-stellar black holes contains a pattern of information made up of hypothetical cosmic mechanisms and established astronomic facts that, combined coherently, explain them well enough to convince us of their existence.

Subjective logic abduction,[1] the most tenuous of the lot, is the "steerage class" means of getting from observation to conclusion, a fallback procedure adopted when the available evidential data is skimpy or non-existent. In this case confirmation must be based on prevailing opinion alone, and in these instances, numerical or symbolic probability values must be attached to each speculative notion advanced in lieu of a known fact.[2]

"Design thinking" is one of the more recent evidence-based techniques and as such, it takes a holistic approach to both thinking and problem-solving in that both the design analyst and the client attempt to view both the problem and the solution simultaneously. This analytic strategy, (one of the precursors of the U-Template methodology), favors the exploration of the problem "environments" as well as the significance of the planner's relative position within their sphere of influence. Relying on "empathy", (seeing the problem through the client's eyes), the appointed designer constructs illuminating analogies or prototypes: objects or illustrations designed to mirror the combined problem/solution in order to generate insight-driven solutions. All in all, design thinking is a one-shot operation where the designer and client conquer the problem together in a comprehensive glance or intuitive *coup de l'oeil*.

According to many, design thinking's holistic approach to problem-solving embraces some of the more productive visual-thinking techniques currently in use. But the question remains: do one-shot visual-thinking procedures

---

1. The U-Template validation process unfolds in accordance with all three abductive inferential processes: that is, according to the accrual of facts, opinions, observations, and well-enlightened guesses.
2. As they are in the U-template and its four emoticons.

actually work?[3] The answer is a guarded "yes". We should be able to trust them—and the feelings of certainty and closure they generate (when they've done the job correctly) at least as fully as we trust the "Aha!" feelings that come over us when, at the tail end of an investigative procedure, we finally "see the whole picture".

3. A Pictorial depiction of a complex idea can provide a special window into its internal organization and coherence in as much as it can be made to fit on a screen or page within narrow spatial limits, (the viewer's visual field), and within easy "eye's reach". Tightly compressed, the conception-cum-picture can now be scanned top to bottom, right and left, backwards and forwards, etc., with an effortless, continuous and free-ranging sweep of the critical eye. This special "shrinkage" treatment is what the U-Template is all about.

CHAPTER 3

THE FINAL STEP IN THE BATTLE
AGAINST UNCERTAINTY

If I'd asked my customers what they wanted, they would
have said 'a faster horse'— *Henry Ford*

Before we leave the subject of verification well behind us,
let's stop for a moment to consider the other side of the
coin—uncertainty and its accompanying states of mind,
especially, (given the nature of this book), the skittish-
ness we feel when debating with ourselves whether or not
to invest our time and resources in the development of
one or more of our bright ideas. Whether we think of
uncertainty as a state of affairs or a psychological condition, we can agree that it often originates in a relatively
simple knowledge (or self-knowledge) gap of some kind.
But when uncertainty stems from something more than
the missing piece of a certain puzzle, that is, when it's
triggered by something far too alien to get-one's-head-
around, we refer to instances of this larger gap as ontological uncertainty. Put simply, it's what makes it harder
for those who have extremely novel and so-called "dis-
ruptive" ideas (e.g., the Ford Model T) to get others to buy
into them as easily as they might accept those of the gar-
den variety. In short, the innovator must make palpable

what is for the moment incomprehensible... and possibly a bit frightening.

... where the knower is part of the knowledge

However, ontological uncertainty can also work in the innovator's favor. It can spur us on well past ordinary cognition, beyond the linear and unidirectional mental processes we normally direct outward toward the world

or inward toward the self. Yes, one-way thinking and/
or knowledge helps us get through the day, but any psychic material springing from this relatively simple realm
of knowledge is, to a certain degree, what-is-already-
known-only-more-of-the-same. Seen through conventional perspectives, this knowledge is already "out there"
somewhere, waiting to be discovered and dragged back
into the familiarity of our private and public cognitive
domains. No great shakes.

According to Gregory Bateson, straight-arrow thinking
will never turn the world upside down à la Copernicus
or Einstein—which for many of us is just fine. In times
of rapid change, there are those of us who'd prefer things
to stay pretty much the same, our lives undisturbed by
mind-bending Unknowns trying to elbow their way into
our consciousness. Perhaps for this reason alone, Bateson's universe is often perceived as something most of us
might want to step around {as lightly as possible) with an
apologetic "I just can't afford all this ... at least not for
now, maybe later, etc." But for those of you who might
like to give this advanced thinking a try, read on, for what
Bateson has to say about meta-knowledge, meta-cogni-
tion, and the power of "recursive" thinking might be just
for you.

Bateson, a polymath scientist and systems theorist, developed a meta-science of his own, the study of thinking-
about-thinking, which he soon added to his own scientific outlook and explorations. Recursive cognition, just
one of a number of his compelling ideas, speaks of a
new, second-tier level of thinking where, as in quantum
mechanics, the observer and observed operate within a
single theoretical and operative system. In practical
terms, it's where the knower is part of the knowledge, a

knowledge that reflects back to the knower both its epistemological content and, most significantly, a glimmer of the manner in which it was produced. And Yes, it's the kind of knowledge that makes innovators.

Bateson was mainly interested in why and how the thinking process and the knowledge base that supports it feed back and forth into each other as accommodatingly as they do. He concluded that under the right conditions, thinking-as-a-function ordinarily adapts effectively to changes in thinking-as-form, and when a new mode of thinking is called for at the appearance of a newly emergent form of knowledge, thinking evolves accordingly, transforming itself to suit the novelty of the new situation. This wholesale conversion then generates new and challenging thought/thinking paradigms that, in turn, spawn entire higher-order thinking systems. Just think about Einstein's innovative use of the word "relativity" and the myriad ways in which its world-wide circulation transformed our thinking style—for better or worse, according to where you stand—into one which cautions us to make non-judgmental appraisals of styles and practices other than our own.

Bateson argues that under these recursive conditions, namely, the back-and-forth communication between process and content, *not* knowing something often works to serve our best interests. The reason? When engaged in recursive thinking, the mind may be animated by the discontinuity between what is known and what is not, and consequently the knowledge gap "attracts attention" to itself. If you read ahead to the section on systems dynamics, you'll recognize that recursion is by nature a self-organizing and self-transformative process. It's also characteristically emergent and produces bright ideas.

CHAPTER 4

HEIGHTEN YOUR LEVEL OF SITUATION AWARENESS

… it's the question business and military leaders ask and often, somehow or other, answer themselves. It's the simple, "Where do I stand right now?"

Okay. Now that we've knocked linear thinking and presented some of its shortcomings, what do we have left? If traditional serial-order rationality won't help us, what in the—real world—*will*?

Good question. And I'll answer it with another question, one that we've had to ask ourselves ever since our primate ancestors first felt bewilderment as to the nature of their surrounding world and how not to let it get the better of them. It's the same question that business and military leaders ask and then, somehow or other, manage to answer themselves. It's the first half of a basic self-positioning Q and A, "Where do I stand right now?" Simple question? Maybe. Maybe not. We'll get to this later.

At any rate, this advanced level of self-orientation, this firm grasp of both our immediate and up-and-coming circumstances known as "situation awareness exemplifies the kind of comprehensive perthinking that allows us to see through the surface of things, through financial markets and battlefields, deep down to their profoundest indications for the immediate and long-term future. As a human faculty it's the exceptional knack for incorporating facts on the ground (including the other guy's perception of that same ground) into a deep and farsighted perspective. It's about staying on top of things, so that nothing untoward is likely to happen that we hadn't already prepared for twice over.

Quite often, our situation awareness comes upon us in piercing flashes of insight, where both the problem and the solution appear suddenly and in rapidly successive stages: perception, interpretation and prediction. In the military, this demonstration of cerebral agility is often referred to as a *coup de l'oeil* or the stroke of the eye. To the tactician Carl von Clausewitz, it was "the ability to see the whole business of war". According to General Frederick Franks, it's "seeing what is now, visualizing the future state of what needs to be done to accomplish the mission".

"That's all well and good," you may reply. "Successful strategies may very well hinge on the level of one's, um, situation awareness. But how does this stuff help me, Joe the plumber? How do I get the hang of it?"

First answer: Practice, practice, practice.

We are all naturally situationally-aware to one degree or another, and with practice, we get better at it. Dynamically, it's all about the parallel processing—of knowledge—we engage in constantly and as a matter of course. Have you ever arranged a bouquet of flowers? This is parallel processing on a conscious level. Have you ever put together a seating plan for a table of dinner guests? This is also cognizant parallel processing. Although this native ability to perthink in parallel is yet to be fully understood, psychologists agree that it's closely associated with our working memory, that handy mental short-term storage system that allows us to turn our attention away from our current thoughts to something else entirely without losing the plot. Surely you can remember times in your life when you had to keep certain thoughts running somewhere in the back of your mind while you directed your chief focus to some other matter. Perhaps you were studiously attending to a colleague's presentation while at the same time you were busy formulating a probing question or clever rebuttal.

Our ability to focus simultaneously on (a) our own thoughts, (b) someone else's thoughts, and (c) subject matter common to both, has about 30 seconds of mnemonic "working" time before the material we've been cradling is transferred to our long-term memory and stowed away for a lengthy period of time. An immediate access to material stored in our short-term memory provides at least two distinct benefits: first, it allows sensory input to be re-evaluated in the light of our more recent experiences, and second, it organizes this information in such a way that we can continually re-establish our position on various matters with regard to our changing circumstances.

But getting back to the question of situation awareness in everyday life: laboratory studies indicate that with practice, we become far more adept at the art of environmental information-extraction. With experience, we sharpen our capacity to classify things as we learn to make better distinctions between more-or-less similar perceptions and when appropriate, to make useful generalizations by learning to ignore currently insignificant differences. All in all, we develop a sharpened ability to recognize meaningful patterns, such as the strategic patterns of attack employed in a chess match or the patterns of light and darkness—indicating health or pathology—captured on an x-ray. Finally, we learn to recognize patterns of emotional experience (which is why, when hearing about a friend's highly personal and distinctive problems, we might think to ourselves, "I've been there").

Of course, what we finally "see" under any set of circumstances will be limited to that-which-we-attend-to as dictated by our own personal needs, select groups of stimuli (signals) that we cull—automatically or purposely—from a vast universe of irrelevancies (noise). Which raises still another how-do-we-do-it question, namely, how do we manage to separate the weighty from the trivial? Not a small concern considering that we receive ninety percent of our received information through our eyes, and having picked up raw sensory material from the retina, all we (the cortex) need to "see"—and only for an instant—are disembodied patterns of light, darkness, color, etc. We don't "create pictures" until the brain has finished arranging every bit of this raw material into readily available perceptual formations.

But despite all this, all the intricacies of our sensory coding and de-coding processes, we do nevertheless manage to assign "weight" well-enough for our immediate purposes. As time goes by and the brain adapts to the natural world, it somehow separates the significant from the incidental with increasing effectiveness.

CHAPTER 5

SHORE UP YOUR SITUATION AWARENESS WITH VISUAL TOOLS

U ntil now, we've been looking at perception, cognition and how, knit closely together, these two psychic mechanisms establish and broaden our familiarity with the physical world. But what about our perception of the non-material world? How do we process disembodied ideas—often formulated by others—that are spelled out for us symbolically "on paper"? While there are those that can easily juggle this type of information (ideas, sub-ideas, connecting ideas, etc.) in-their-heads so to speak, the rest of us tend to require outside assistance. And when it all gets too much for us, we often turn to graphic organizers.

A graphic organizer (see below) is an information storage/display system that portrays complex information architecturally within an organized visual field, and when expressed structurally, the same idea can reveal itself far better than it might were it presented otherwise, e.g., sentence-by-sentence. But to understand spatial organization as it applies to the graphic presentation of idea-complexes, we must first understand what we mean when we speak of an idea's "architectural" properties.

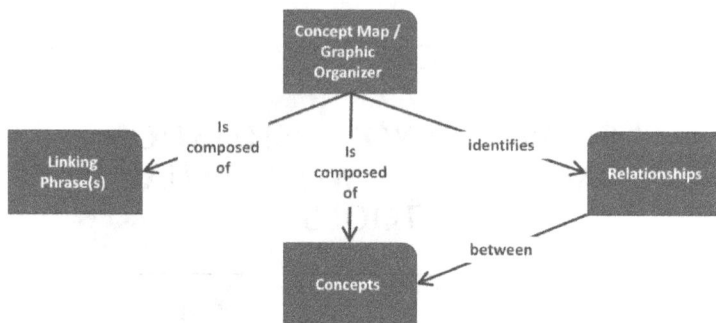

To start with, there are many types of idea-structures floating out there in the ether, some of them more amenable to diagrammatic representation than others. Nevertheless, their structural attributes all serve one definite purpose or another. There's the Aristotelian dramatic narrative structure involving the plot as a whole and its tripartite division of (setting), middle (action), and end (resolution), a structure common to many other literary forms as well. Then there are other, more complicated structures, idea "packages" such as, in descending order, generalization, concept, topic, fact. There's also the logical argument structure (e.g., All As are Bs, C is B, and therefore, C is A); musical structures such as the sonata form (i.e. exposition, development, and recapitulation), and the classic 32-bar AABA pop tune form (theme, same theme again, another theme, initial theme).

One of the earliest attempts to structure knowledge architecturally was mathematician and philosopher Gottfried Wilhelm von Leibniz, who attempted to find a single visual framework designed to tie together a wide variety of concepts. Leibniz didn't get very far with this pro-

Leibnitz's pictogram, an early attempt to structure knowledge architecturally

ject and the pictogram shown—portraying Leibniz's belief that all earthly things are made up of different combinations of earth, water, air, and fire—is one of the two graphic images he constructed in his lifetime.

According to Leibniz and many others who followed him, all ideas and concepts are nothing but combinations of ideational and conceptual subsets. Leibniz's visual alphabet would, in theory, provide a means of enhancing our analytic-thinking processes methodically with broad concepts reduced to their elemental parts. (The natural outgrowth of this position is the notion, still in currency, that many of the Big Concepts of today are merely practical assemblages of ideas that circulated yesterday.) So here we have our first specific idea-structure worth mentioning: ideas comprised of other ideas somewhat older and narrower than themselves.

... he was banking on the immense power of the "eye's mind", the part of our mental apparatus most sensitive to the spatial properties of incoming patterns of information.

Question: So why did Leibniz feel that ideas depicted architecturally might take on meanings—i.e. in the form of explicit relationships—that would otherwise remain well out of our reach? Answer: he was banking on the immense power of the "eye's mind," the part of our mental apparatus most sensitive to the spatial properties of incoming patterns of information such as those that convey distance, position and size, which receives them, processes them, and finally comes up with its own "take" on the nature of their source. Whether he knew it or not, Leibnitz was on to something very big. The fact is that before we fully perceive objects, the brain picks up on a limited number of their rudimentary visual properties and registers them momentarily for further processing an instant later. Which is to our great advantage. Once this initial pre-conscious selection process has done its job capturing basic information instantly, the mind is free to do other, perhaps more important, things: such as when primitive man had to decide, "Is this thing something I should run from?" or, "Is this something I should chase down and have for lunch?"

NAILING DOWN THE SITUATION—PAST, PRESENT, AND FUTURE—WITH CONCEPT MAPS

John Dewey wrote, "It is a familiar and significant saying that a problem well -put is half solved. To find out what the problem and problems are which a problematic situation presents to be inquired into, is to be well along in (the) inquiry." Indeed. If a concept map, just one of a wide variety of graphic organizers, is well- assembled, it can capture a complex idea, its diverse elements, and the interrelationships that bind its component parts to each other in such a way that that, yes, the problem is often half solved.

All in all, graphic organizers are man-made information reception-storage-display systems that organize knowledge very much the way the visual cortex does: by portraying complex information spatially and architecturally. The concept map, one of the more popular of these visual tools, sheds light on our ideas by illustrating the manner in which they might be seen within a common conceptual context. These items are depicted spatially in proximal positions representing "closeness" of association and, specifically, vertical positions for hierarchal status. Arrows are often used to represent the nature of the connections (such as A is the cause of B, C is dependent on D, etc.). When concept maps are used to uncover the interrelationship of ideas broad enough to embrace entire business or life-change strategies, they can, on occasion, reveal personal perspectives or expose gaps—or twists—in a specific line of reasoning. You might say that concept maps approach complex ideas in much the same way that a (wise) blind man, upon encountering an elephant and curious as to "the nature of the beast," might explore its bodily parts while circling the animal and making a mental note of everything that presents itself to the touch—e.g., trunk, tail, ears, etc.—with an unbroken sweep of the hand (and mind).[1]

Finally—and here's where the U-Template begins to fit into the picture—a concept map can organize business or personal plans by conveying a sense of the temporal flow of an operation: now the problem, soon working on the problem and still later, defeating the problem by reaching the objective. The U-Template is an entirely new instru-

---

1. At this juncture, I should clarify how and why a (loaded) U-Template differs significantly from a (completed) mind map. Although they are similar in respect to their dependence on words and word associations, they are worlds apart in form and function. The mind map is built on tree structures and radial hierarchies connected by loose word associations, i.e., key words that express whatever comes immediately to one's mind. The nature of the relationships between key words will rarely be apparent if it's ever necessary to review the associations responsible for the internal logic of the map. Of course, mind maps are often intuitive, creative, and leading the way to brilliant solutions, but again, they will rarely be self-validating and are not likely to indicate whether or not the mind-mapped idea, if it's a plan of action, is worth the gamble.

ment, a concept map that depicts both the form and function of an idea-in-development as it might play out in a hypothetical problem environment. It's a multi-purpose direction-finder that speaks to where we are, where we want to go, and, finally, the route we should take to get there (in one piece).

The U-Template organizes project-relevant key words within a set of contiguous spaces organized by project-related function and standards of judgment. With the help of this multi- function and multi-criteria arrangement, it can depict the visual landscape of the most complex and extensive business/institutional or personal life-change plan.[2] Two questions will routinely emerge from the finalized display:

- Will this concept map help the planner fully appreciate an idea's structure and dynamics?

- Will this visual image reveal new patterns of meaning that have a bearing on the plan's ultimate validity?

---

2. When dealing with problems that are of a multi-factor nature—as they are in business or in government—the choice of a suitable solution among many alternatives is rather subjective (i.e., made on the basis of unarticulated "druthers"). This variety of multi-criteria decision analysis, or MCDA, is often employed to allow decision-makers to state their preferences factor-by- factor and criterion-by-criterion. In the typical MCDA process, a set of current objectives (e.g., what we need to achieve in order to solve problem x) are specified, followed by the selection of several alternative actions (and the criteria required to judge and compare them) that are likely to meet these objectives. All in all, the decision-making process is divided into increasingly smaller units (to be decided upon piecemeal, in serial order and outside of a larger context. These traditional MCDA procedures often produce ambiguous, conflicting, or incompatible scores which are then compressed into a single number representing the "best solution". (But can we be assured that the alternatives are weighted properly if at all, and that "best" translates into "good enough"?)

CHAPTER 6

THE UNIVERSAL TEMPLATE

O K, enough theory for the present. Welcome to the U-Template. It's a new and fairly unique device, so to ensure that you get a reasonable sense of what it's all about, I'll start with this riddle: "Why is a good idea like a good sandwich?" Can't guess? Well, let me ask you this: Have you ever sat in a restaurant and noticed some other patron gazing regretfully at her plate, as if choosing that particular item from the menu maybe wasn't such a good idea? The truth is that unfamiliar dishes, when we're not quite prepared for them, can put us off big-time, even when it's only a sandwich (and it looks like nothing we've ever seen before). This sense of dire confrontation is what it might feel like to confront an idea unlike anything we've ever *thought* before (even if the idea is our own brainchild). But a sandwich or an idea that seems unnervingly foreign at first glance shouldn't stop us from giving it at least a casual try. On the contrary, we may have stumbled upon something gloriously inventive and satisfying. So, sit down and have a sandwich. An Idea Sandwich. Conceived and assembled for the sole purpose of feeding the curious animal in all of us.

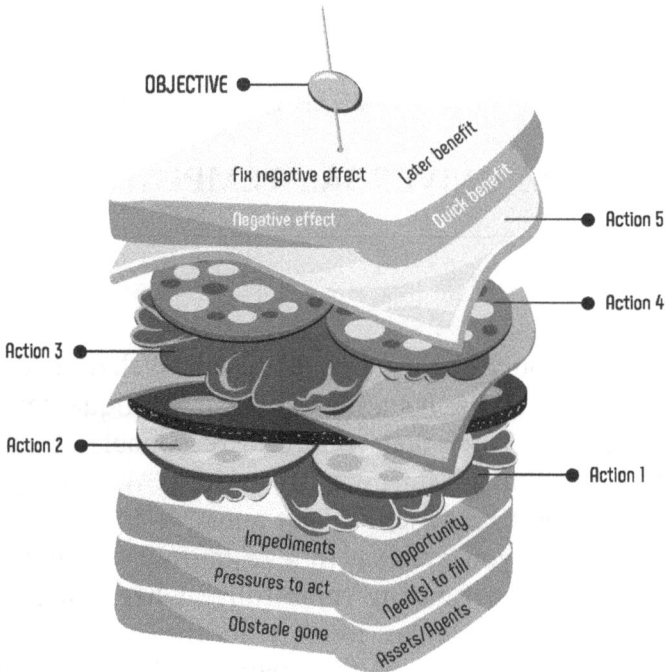

The idea sandwich

The Universal Template will be our sandwich *du jour* and, to continue in the parlance of the kitchen:

- It will provide "food for thought".

- It can be "tasted" in one flavorsome "bite".

- It will consist of a "wrapping" with various "fillings" and "garnishes".

- When mixed together in the proper amounts, the sandwich's (here the template's) own "textures" (hard facts) and "flavors" (soft abstract principles) will provide just the right fare for the curious and imaginative mind.

Finally, just as a master chef takes care to arrange the food on your plate into sensible portions, the U-Template organizes your ideas (including their supporting facts, opinions, best guesses, etc.) as quickly as they pile up in your mind, and in doing so, reduces any possible information-overload to a manageable number of recognizable "chunks".

Project Name- The Ford Model T , Status- Open , Author- DEMO
View : My Plan | Edit Primary Text | Add + Revise raw data, hi-specific items, final afterthoughts
Invite Guests | Tallied Foundations/Fulfilments | Tallied Actions | Overall Vote | Guests Status

Click here to see how to use My Plan

Fulfilments

OBJECTIVE		The Ford Model T, A friendly car	
FIX NGTVE EFFECT	Satisfy workers, Better public relations	LATER BENEFIT	Market share, prestige, Make history
NEGATIVE EFFECT	Shock, Confusion, Resistance	QUICK BENEFIT	Greater profits, New factory+dealerships

Actions

Infuse more capital

Failure? Steel, Fuel+water systems

Road test

Sort out OK, NOT OK components.

Assemble components, new hoist system.

Build, test components

Review blueprint+design

Create design to blueprint.

Formulate simple blueprint

Foundations

IMPEDIMENTS	Profit slowdown,Snobbery,Roads	OPPORTUNITY	Travel revolution-- commuters, shoppers.
PRESSURES TO ACT	Other cheap cars, Profit pressure	NEED(S)TO FILL	Friendly, cheap, car
OBSTACLE GONE	Selden patent, Conservative stockholder	ASSETS/AGENTS	Our team, Kent Smith, Vanadium steel

Click on Blue keywords to view any remaining words.
Mouse over the black labels for a better sense of their meaning.
Guests - Click the blue keywords to submit comments via text and symbols.

How to review your ideas   Revise Display

U-Template screen

So what exactly is the U-Template? Let's say that you've been thinking about making some significant changes in your life or business. You've already whipped up a few rudimentary ideas to this end, just a rough mental sketch of your current problems and how things might improve if you decide to tackle them in the near future. But that's all you've got. You still don't have a fully developed idea of what would be required to get the job done and whether or not you alone and/or your associates are up to the job.

Finally, after endless passive speculation, you realize that your thoughts will remain jumbled and disjointed as long as they remain bottled up in the dark and cobwebbed corners of your mind. So, you finally commit your plan—such as it is—to paper, word after word, sentence after sentence, half-baked idea after half-baked idea, hoping to view it more objectively and through an enlightening perspective. But having spelled it all out on the page and having had a good look at what you've got so far, are you any the wiser? Do you see anything new in this pile of written material? Yes, possibly, but it's just as likely that no matter how many times you'll continue to pore over these strings of grammatically-correct, serial-order prose, your ideas will come back at you exactly as you set them down, still withholding their deep secrets as stubbornly as before. Wordiness, grammatical form and the limitations of the human mind (the working memory needed to hold down and cross-inspect the salient factors) will continue to get the better of you.

But imagine that in a last-ditch effort to see your ideas for what they may prove to be at the end of the road, you decide to free them from the standard prose in which you've encased them, and reversing your tactics, you reduce them to key words spread out in some other, non-grammatical order[1], (herded into a convenient mental holding pen). You've now created a conceptual "thinking space" in which your idea fragments—and others that might come to mind—can be sorted and consolidated

---

1. Which is why the U-Template offers the use of its doubt-denoting emoticons.

into a suitable plan of action with the help of a special diagram, the U-Template, designed to accommodate your ideas according to how they might work together in the context of an organized plan. You are now able to review your idea and its particulars as they lie there embedded in a single design, the same way you might examine a fine painting (first as an integral whole, soon after in accordance with its salient features and finally through its minutia, detail by detail), poring over the material every which way so as to extract as much substance from the material as it has to give. Now, scanning these key words every which way your eyes take you, has your plan been exposed to the light of day? [2]

To sum up: The U-template is an effective, one-size-fits-all testing platform for the resolution of project-driven issues. Consistent with the assumption that complex matters are rarely simplified by correspondingly complex models, the U-Template's skeletal architecture structures and reduces to their barest essence of both author input (as data) and viewer output (as conceptualization). The template's one-screen display system, the first of several subsequent windows to appear in the course of the analytic procedure, permits project collaborators to visually scan an entire action plan, (all major items and their appropriate assessment criteria) with one uninterrupted sweep of the eye, in much the same way that one might consider the opportunities and hazards of a difficult chess match. With help of the U-Template, planners are finally able to view and consider all possible "thinking points"

2. Similarly, additional contextual meanings are provided by the U-Template's three-fold past-present-future narrative, its ten criteria, its qualifiers (emoticons), and finally its organizing/unifying "Bright Idea", i.e., the Objective.

and beyond to the big picture, the all-important "why" behind it all.

LEVELS OF THE U-TEMPLATE

The U-template engages the user on three different levels of analytic thinking.

The first level contains the basic plan according to its own spatial logic. Compressed onto a single screen, the project elements displayed here allow the viewer to adopt a wide perspective and eventually determine whether or not the overall plan is viable.

The **second level** (of the corporate model), conveyed electronically to each associate viewer along with levels one and three, allows the originator to communicate his/her ideas in greater detail. In addition to capturing and conveying the originator's initial ideas, all input fields provide room for commentary to be contributed by all recipient participants. Collaborator feedback and open discussion accumulates, creating an opinion board pertaining to each and every issue alluded to on the level one and the subsequent relevant commentary. This system affords originators and recipients the opportunity to identify the specific elements of the proposal that have incurred particular favor or disfavor.

The **third level**—of the corporate model—accommodates illustrations and specifications central to the idea-originator's proposal.

There is also a **fourth level**, a final screen providing a visual analysis of all that's gone before. This overview, expressed in a series of charts and graphs, describes all previous collaborator inputs from a number of different perspectives.

A DEEPER LOOK AT THE SURFACE LEVEL

Level One, the template surface, is divided into three main sections: foundations, actions and fulfilments.

FOUNDATIONS

Listed at the bottom of the U-Template are six key judgmental criteria that both the idea-originator and project team need to take into consideration as the plan is constructed and reviewed. Specifically, this information describes significant past and present conditions within the organization's internal and external environments and helps to support or oppose the argument for the implementation of the plan. As many of these conditions have been built on past mistakes, we do well to keep in mind the old admonition, "those that remember the past are bound to repeat it."

The six judgmental criteria that form the foundations' subsections are:

Assets/Agents. In this field, the project team identifies the critical resources (i.e., people, skills and know-how, technologies, materials and equipment, capital, etc.) that must be made available to support the project. In doing so, the team will begin to appreciate the project's practical interdependencies and the potential risks attendant with any failure to obtain these critical resources from key sponsors and stakeholders.

Need(s) to Fill. In this field, the team identifies the needs of the marketplace and/or the organization that the project is meant to satisfy. This review should answer the question, "How is this project enriching the lives of those who the project architects must keep in mind as they develop a new product or service for their benefit?" In the long run, the team needs to recognize what does or does not constitute value, a question that builds and maintains a strong linkage between the project and the real world.

Opportunities. There may be environmental or inner-organizational opportunities opening up that the project team would be exploiting in following the proposed plan. In this regard, the team needs to address these positive contingencies early in the planning process, perhaps so early that the project would not be altogether conceivable until the opportunity in question made itself fully known.

Impediments to Progress. In this field, the team identifies those existing internal or external obstructions (such as affordability, costs, difficulties with the time-line, ever-shifting environmental conditions, competition, or resistance from biased or misinformed organizational insiders etc.), that can potentially limit or retard the development of the project. These adverse current and/or near-future difficulties, often ignored by project enthusiasts, may prove to be too formidable to resolve. Consequently, the project team must carefully assess the dimensions of these problematic factors well before the conclusion of the planning process.

Pressures to Act. Many projects are built upon a foundation of circumstances that seem to demand quick and unconditional action. But very often, the pressure itself is almost entirely psychological and based on dubious forecasts of upcoming crises or providential cash cows. In this input field, internal or external factors that strongly demand that the current project be initiated are identified and perhaps questioned. As long as the prevailing sense of urgency is well-founded and the case for action remains valid, there may be no cause for hesitancy. But if such pressures subside quickly, too quickly to be legitimate, then it may be time to call for a review of the project's overall validity and its specific business case.

Obstacle(s) Gone. As far as the U-Template is concerned, these identified obstacles are past problems that no longer constrain the organization. The responses in this field will identify those project-defeating barriers, if any, that once exhibited resistance to the project, but had to be surmounted before the project could get underway. If the obstacle was related to the objections of reluctant project sponsors or champions, paying attention to those who now support the project and *why* they do so will have an enormous bearing on how and why the project needs to be undertaken.

ACTIONS

Listed in this section are the practical steps that need to be taken to reach the plan's main objective, along with expressions of concern, item by item, as to the possibility of one or more weaknesses or unfavorable consequences of each action and the corrective measures that may need to be taken immediately or soon after.

Actions appear mid-page. Each action is annotated with one of a series of emoticons as follows: (1) Positive action: OK; (2) Consequence of an earlier action: (a) Non-OK but fixable consequence or, (b) High risk consequence (respectively green, light gray, dark gray, and red, with expressions ranging from a broad smile to a deep frown).

OBJECTIVE

This title refers to the project's immediate outcome; the embodiment of the bright idea that will drive the project forward and differentiates this projected outcome from subsequent matters, e.g., short term benefits that should arise once the objective has been reached.

FULFILMENTS

Listed here are the potential benefits that might follow from the achievement of the main objective and reflect the motivational forces driving the plan. Possible negative consequences of the plan as a whole are also indicated here, as are the actions required to counteract them if they do materialize. Too many anticipated negative consequences may suggest a full overhaul or complete abandonment of the plan and the project.

There are four subsections of Fulfilments that deal with the potential benefits and negative consequences.

Short-Term (Quick) Benefits. This section of the U-Template identifies those immediate benefits that can be expected subsequent to the project's completion, the rewards that will justify the struggle to attain the plan's objective.

The specific benefits may include:

- The advancement of company capability and influence (including a better position vis-à-vis competitors) along with all material benefits.

- The commencement of the project profit flow and the replenishment of resources spent on investment costs.

- A trans-organizational learning experience, morale

boosts and the satisfaction of producing something beneficial for oneself and others.

Long-Term (Later) Benefits. This section identifies the likely organizational benefits, related to growth as well as material reward, that can be expected to occur relatively late in the project time frame, either as a direct result of reaching the project's objective, or as a secondary benefit arising from earlier post-project gains. Very often these ancillary rewards are left out of the go/no-go equation, resulting in missed opportunities. These benefits are commonly anticipated and spelled-out by team leaders whose job it is to think more broadly with an eye open to future patterns and trends in the marketplace. These long-term forecasts usually anticipate tomorrow's model, and for this reason, they are not always terribly clear to the uninitiated, who must be briefed on these matters from time to time.

Potential Negative Effects. Here the project's author/idea originator mentions the possible occurrence of one or more unfavorable project outcomes and describes their likely negative impact. The extent to which these leaders recognize these possible negative outcomes will determine the team's ability to make planning adjustments in response. Pertinent issues might include:

1. Will these events retard the growth of the organization?
2. Might they force us to shut down entirely?
3. Might they simply outweigh the project's expected long- and short-term benefits?

Fix Negative Effects. This assessment serves as the basis for anticipating potential courses of corrective action that might conceivably be taken by the project team in response to certain unfavorable operational or post-objective occurrences. Once identified on the template, these proposed countermeasures can be communicated to all outside stakeholders so as to best influence their initial expectations and avoid any potentially adverse reactions to necessary last-minute ad hoc deviations from the original plan. Naturally, resources should be budgeted for all such contingencies.

Questions that might arise in response to these warnings include:

- Will we have sufficient resources to go on despite these adversities?
- Can we develop resources to compensate for them, e.g., learning and implementing new production methods or service techniques?

Can we use the experience gained in the course of the project to counteract the trends that led to these undesirable outcomes?

CHAPTER 7

A DEMONSTRATION OF THE U-TEMPLATE IN ACTION

THE FORD MODEL T EXAMPLE

To illustrate how to complete a U-Template, we will use details of the Ford Model T sample (also to be found in the hands-on U-Template software application you will soon use to assess one of your own ideas). This specimen should give you some idea of how a U-Template should look upon its completion.

It shows you how the U-Template will allow you, the initial project planner/idea originator, to outline a step-by-step action plan which the program will spell out within the limits of a single screen. You will be prompted to answer a series of standard questions in connection with the plan's major and minor features.

You simply answer all questions intelligently using key words, or responding with "unsure at this stage" or "doesn't apply" if necessary. This is all that will be required of you, the software will do the rest. You are then free to browse the template at will. If you decide to make changes, just click the Revise Display button to bring up the questions again for more appropriate responses.

To access the U-Template application and our Ford Model T example:

1. Go to **www.u-template.com**
2. Select Demo > Business
3. Select a Project, select The Ford Model T
4. Click Review

SOME PRELIMINARY CONCEPTS

Let's start with the important terms and concepts you'll need. We'll illustrate them with data from the Ford Model T example.

THE USERS

The Author-Originator

The idea-originator constructs a U-Template in order to explain the idea to others in such a way that there is little doubt as to how or why the idea should be expanded into a fully-developed product or service. As an integral part of an electronic meeting process, the originator fills out the idea on the template, ensuring that all recipient reactions to the diagram are direct, appropriate, and constructive.

The Recipient

The recipient/collaborator has been invited to the meeting by the originator to help review the U-Template display. These meeting attendees are presumed to have little or no previous familiarity with the idea, but at least a general knowledge of the project environment in which the idea will be actualized.

FOUNDATIONS

The foundations section, appropriately enough, is

displayed at the bottom of the U-Template screen. These describe 'positive' (Opportunities, Need(s) to fill, Assets/agents) and 'negative' elements of the project (Impediments, Pressures to act, Obstacles).

ASSETS/AGENTS

Our resources, human or material, immediate or potential.

Example: Ford identifies his personnel, materials, and systems.

> *Our design team, Charley Sorensen, Harold Wills, and Joe Galamb, is the best in the business. I have a lot of faith in them. I believe our improved light-weight vanadium steel alloy is going to stand up over all the jolts of the worst roads. Finally, our assembly line, although not yet perfect, will benefit from the new hoists I intend to include—this means less lifting and more output per worker.*

Key words: Design team, vanadium steel, assembly line.

PRESSURES TO ACT

Alarm bells calling for action.

Example: Ford identifies economic pressures.

> *I'm afraid we may lose market share to one of the other Big Four companies. A few of them have put*

out some cheaper models, and even though they haven't sold all that well, somebody may come along and beat me to the first really cheap car. Our stockholders want greater profits and I think the only way we can double or triple our profits is to build a car almost anyone can afford.

Key words: Competition, stockholders.

IMPEDIMENTS TO PROGRESS

Potential problems lying before us that could slow us down or make things difficult.

Example: Ford identifies logistical and psychological impediments.

I'm concerned about the limited space in our present plant. I'm tired of bringing materials into one space and then assembling parts in another. We should be carrying out all operations under one roof. My other concern is the never-ending consumer resistance to "cheap" cars. They think you've got to spend big bucks to buy yourself a decent car.

Key words: Limited space, consumers.

NEEDS TO FILL

Filling these needs (the world's or ours) will serve us.

Example: Ford identifies practical and psychological consumer needs.

No matter what anybody thinks, I know that a "friendly" car will sell like hotcakes. What are the consumer's real needs? For a safer car (left hand drive). For maneuverability on bad roads. For a car they can sometimes fix themselves, with a screwdriver, a little bit of wire, etc. For a car they can trust.

Key words: Cheap, friendly car.

OPPORTUNITIES

A shift in internal or external conditions to our advantage.

Example: Ford identifies favorable socio-economic trends.

Things out there are changing a mile a minute. Housewives are becoming independent and want to travel to the shops by themselves. Small businesses are getting bigger every day, and owners want to make their "rounds" for hundreds of miles. There's a huge urban swing to the suburbs, and professional people are going to want to commute back and forth from the city on their own schedules.

Key words: Socio-economic revolution.

NO LONGER OBSTACLES

Conditions, once constraining us, have changed for the better, and we can now act.

Example: Ford identifies a past problem which no longer exists.

> *I am pleased to report that we can now move ahead with my plan for a cheap mass-produced car without having to worry about trouble from inside the company. You all know there was resistance from Malcomson. Well that's all over and done with now. He's out of the picture.*

Key words: Reluctant stockholder.

A QUICK TOUR OF U-TEMPLATE USING THE FORD EXAMPLE

Now that you have studied the Ford Model T project, you will see how the U-Template software can be used to assess a tentative project.

So now try the following.

LEVEL ONE TOUR

You'll notice a gray bar on the left of the opening screen that highlights the three Level One sections: (from the bottom) Foundations, Actions and Fulfilments.

At the top of the main opening screen, you'll see a

menu that provides more detailed views and takes
you further into Levels Two and Three.

1. **Scan back and forth over the template**. Ford's
   plan, in key words, progresses from bottom to
   top. Notice how, in Ford's case, all the criteria
   and operations are more or less consistent and
   little has been left to chance.
2. **Fix (Negative) Effect**. Click the key words to
   the right of the label as a sample of all second-
   tier screens. Notice that the input text spells
   out all that has been implied by its associated
   key word. Notice that a number of guests have
   supplied commentary on this one issue,
   accompanied by a vote indicating their level of
   agreement.
3. **Click Visual Input**. This is the third-tier field
   where Ford, the idea originator, has
   occasionally supplied documentation to
   illustrate or support his case.
4. **Click Tallied Foundations/Fulfillments**. The
   arrows indicate the extent to which all guests
   had confidence in the soundness of the issues
   upon which they were commenting. For
   instance, Ford's views on the significance of
   the Selden patents gave credence to the idea
   that Ford's objective (the Model T) was
   obtainable despite the legal barrier.
5. **Click Tallied Actions**. This is a reflection of
   guest input regarding confidence in the

feasibility of the plan-step and repeats in aggregate what we saw earlier on the second tier.

6. **Click Overall Vote**. The chart on the left represents total guest agreement and disagreement on all the conditions and steps to be taken. The chart on the right represents the guest's overall feelings about the plan, no matter what he or she has indicated, issue by issue.

7. **Click Edit Primary Text** to view the various initial idea-originator input fields.

USING EMOTICONS TO EXPRESS DOUBT AND
AGREEMENT

We will now delve into the Action Drivers to show you how the emoticons can be used to express doubt or agreement.[1]

There are four emoticons—rudimentary symbols that represent a range of author uncertainties, from strong doubt to relative confidence regarding the relative value and do-ability of one or more of the operational stages you have listed on the template. Ask yourself, "can this be done? Will the action move the project forward?" Where your chosen emoticons indicate that the majority of your expectations seem relatively shaky, the plan in its entirety is likely to be flawed and

1. See "Random thoughts on expressing doubt", pg. 124

unsound, and it may be that you're barking up the wrong tree. If so, it might be time to rethink your expectations and, more specifically, to do some serious thinking about your basic premises.

Try the following exercise.

1. In the top menu, click Edit Primary Text (or click the Revise Display button on the bottom right of the screen)
2. Select item 3 Action Drivers
3. Review each action and the four emoticons (positive, OK, non-OK and High risk)

Notice that for each action, there is a box to describe the action, a key word field, and one of four emoticons that can be applied to vote for or rate the action.

Here are some Actions from the Ford Model T example.

First Action

Description: The sketches I've made describe the overall conception that will inform all blueprint and design work by the team. All work will be kept absolutely secret to protect my eventual patent ...

Key words: Formulate simple blueprint.

Second Action

Description: In general, the car has to be easy to drive and repair, however ignition comfort will be sacrificed for the sake of reliability, which means that we're going to stick with the hand-crank function. Repair will be made easier with a cleaner oil system ...

Key words: Create design to blueprint.

And so on for the remaining actions.

Notice that the key words also appear on the opening screen in the Actions section. Clicking on a key word link will show you the action with detailed feedback from all users.

CHAPTER 8

ADVANCED TIPS

N ow that you've had a quick tour of the basics, here are some tips to help you understand and use the real power of the U-Template process. Again, we will use the Ford Model T example to demonstrate.

THE RECIPIENT/COLLABORATOR'S PERSPECTIVE

Remember earlier that we introduced the two types of users: the originator and the recipient or collaborator. Up to now we've been using the author of the U-Template as the initial originator of the project. Now let's see how recipients/collaborators can review and contribute to the U-Template.

REVIEWING THE PROJECT

First, read the display from the bottom up (chronologically): Action Foundations, Action Drivers, and Action Fulfillments.

Next, click on all the category headings (e.g., No Longer Obstacles) to bring up all supporting content (e.g., "conditions have changed and we can now act").

Then, click on all originator second-page inputs to uncover further information.

Consider the following issues:

Action Foundations: Are they significant? Do they accurately reflect past and present issues? Do they lend support to the logic of the plan as a whole?

Action Drivers: Do they describe a credible progression of events? Do the unfavorable or "high risk" consequences seem rectifiable as shown on the display? Does the plan seem to have a reasonable chance of success, i.e., of achieving its Objective without incurring (irreversible) unfavorable consequences?

Action Fulfillments: Does it seem likely that having achieved its objective, the project will produce the projected Short-Term Benefits? The Long-Term Benefits? Does it seem that the Negative Consequences of the plan are manageable as described?

Next, scan back and forth between all the elements on the display. Are they compatible? For instance, in the Impediments to Progress (the Ford sample), is it likely that the identified current consumer bias in favor of expensive cars will continue to present a problem for Ford once his Model T and its affordable price have been well advertised?

When you have completed your examination, assume the role of collaborator by double clicking on the material to which you want to respond (to the originator and/or other collaborators), then click on the "Add Comment" button to enter this feedback. You may also respond to comments from other collaborators in the same manner.

You can return to your feedback at some future time to read feedback on your contributions from other collaborators. Finally, if as a critic/collaborator you'd like to alter the display significantly and present a better plan, create a U-Template of your own.

INTERPRETING EMOTICONS

During this recipient/collaborator review process, you will assign emoticons as part of the feedback process. Here is one set of interpretations that you can apply to their use.

- **Red** = Do something about this if you can; it's not right.

- **Green** = You shouldn't have to worry about this.

- **Light Gray** = See if (and how) this item might possibly affect other variables unfavorably.

- **Dark Gray** = This may worry you, but you can fix it.

DOUBLE-LOOP THINKING

Double your thinking with Chris Argyris's double-loop thinking, a bottom-up approach to what might be described as a conceptual overhaul of a stalled project starting with an intensive review of project origins, including:

1. Unexamined or unspoken premises and assumptions (e.g., "we've always done it this way") which may constitute a good part of the root problem
2. Narrow and ineffective strategies that may have been given only minimal attention due to a company policy or some other unspoken constraint

3. Dysfunctional operations which may have originally been diagnosed in bits and pieces in place of ...
4. If indicated by the above, a wholesale rethinking of the problem "starting from letter A" might be advisable.

Double-loop thinking can be applied just as beneficially to projects that are short-sighted for any number of reasons. When things go wrong as a result of constricted views of a forthcoming task, it's always best to double back to the beginning and reflect on the "why" of it all (e.g., Why did I set out to do this in the first place? What is the reason-behind-my-reasoning?). This is actually a comparatively simple thing to do with a U-Template at one's side. One of the reasons that the U-Template method is so inherently self-modifying is that it forces us to review each and every template input again and again in light of the whole plan, and this means we're challenging our working hypotheses, the project's "business case", on a continuing basis.

Consider the Model T for a moment. If Henry Ford hadn't stepped back and taken a good look at his clunky, snail-paced garage-system, he might have remained an obscure maker of "unfriendly" cars, never to achieve his dream of seeing the American Road bustling with carloads of hyper-mobile families. But one good look at his original business model and the (conservative) ideas behind it (that a good car was a heavy, fancy car) and he saw right away that people couldn't really afford (nor did they need) the expensive, gas guzzling juggernauts for which they had been paying big bucks. As a result, his outlook widened, Ford realized that a simpler, cheaper, factory-made car might suit the public just fine. And, of course, the rest is history.

REVIEWING THE FINALIZED TEMPLATE

As a general rule, a good idea has to gestate for a while before it's ready to be delivered to the world as a *fait accompli*, and it might be better to keep your completed template at hand for your own repeated inspection and unveil it publicly only when you're sure that it's been reviewed as thoroughly as possible. When you first examine your completed template, many considerations you hadn't noticed before may now leap at you from the monitor screen. But the more elusive items may need additional time to grab your attention, which is why you must continually consult the template for as long as its contents seem to require. Having done so, you can then approve of the idea, discount it, or return it to the drawing board for a major overhaul.

Of course, you should also double-check your finalized template to determine whether what's up there on the screen matches what's up there in your head and whether your display faithfully represents your Bright Idea both at its core and in its particulars. In doing so you should also be re-assessing the soundness of the idea itself, which is another matter entirely. If it's the idea itself that's failed the test, perhaps it can be redesigned to suit your requirements. If not, maybe you might want to call the whole idea a "miss" and move on to Plan B.

When an idea occurs to you at a time when you're without your laptop, you can construct your own U-Template with just a pencil and paper. But if you decide to alter your template for any purpose whatsoever, do your best to adhere to the U-Template's essential requirements. First, make certain that your diagram is compact enough for the eye to wander round comfortably for an extended period. Secondly, and following from the first, no matter how your new design takes shape, the plan's step-by-step procedure must be enclosed sandwich-like top and bottom between your two sets of bottom success factors. These ten criteria must give your eye's mind the opportunity to apply them to every item on the display. At the same time, each procedural step and its particulars will serve as a point of comparison for all others of its kind (and so they will also serve as some sort of criteria). Arranged in this way, every item on the template should "talk" to all the others with each sweep of the eye.

Most of your project's essential features will be patently interrelated one way or another and to a greater or lesser degree, but one or more elements will appear to be largely superfluous and/or external to the integrated system. Not to worry. Some systems' elements are like that: significant but not necessarily integral. Just let them hang there on the template and in your own thoughts for a while, as they may prove to be strategically important to the project as invaluable "extras". Remember, though, that the interrelationships among the parts of a system, any system, may be one-to-one, one-to several, and several-to-several. Furthermore, these established linkages may serve one or more dynamic purposes, namely amplifying, damping, or, if you've struck gold, "emergence-making".

As you introduce key words to your plan, try to be selective and keep your list of critical actions or operations to twelve or below. You can't anticipate each and every project factor you'll be examining, and if it were possible, you'd soon find yourself struggling with a bad case of information-overload.

Bottom-up approach for confirming the practicality of the project

Although in the Western world we normally read text from top to bottom, the U-Template moves chronologically, i.e., from bottom to top, reflecting its "onward and upward" thrust from Foundations to Fulfilments. You may want to ask yourself:

- Are your foundations sturdy enough to support the entire plan?

- Are the obstacles (if any) that once stood in your way no longer there?

- Do you feel that you can get past your impediments if and when they arise?

- How many "slam dunk" actions can you identify?

- Are there more than a few red or dark gray negative emoticons?

- Do all project particulars seem to serve the Objective?

For the organizational team, a top-down approach to confirming the validity of the project

Ask yourself: Will the project's long- and short-term benefits increase the organization's well-being?

- Will the organization be able to build on the Objective's newly gained advantages?

- Will the experience gathered in the course of the project enhance its knowledge-base and skills?

- Will the completed project serve the organization as an enabler of other projects?

- Might the negative consequences of the project's outcomes prove to be disastrous?

- Do the "fixes" of the unfavorable project outcomes seem to be adequate?

- What might be its full cost in time, energy, and resources?

- Having thought through your project's negative contingencies, do the project's benefits seem to justify the overall risk?

With respect to deciding on whether or not to go forward with your project: if you're not 100% sure you should do so, it is sometimes best to put your mind on hold for a few days. In the interim, you'll be handing over greater control to your intuitive powers, which will continue to decide this question while your conscious mind is focused elsewhere.

Please consider this (factual) scenario of a U-Template review performed recently by a test subject examining the Ford Template. Upon confronting the base template (the surface level), the subject's attention was drawn to the Objective, "the Ford model T, a friendly and affordable car", as part of his initial attempt to get the gist of the plan. To better understand the standard Ford might have set for his car, the subject dug down to the third level, Formulate a Simple Blueprint, to determine whether he would discover a simple vehicle design, and in particular a lightweight chassis. To check further on this matter, he turned to Build and Test Components to learn more about the chassis, which as illustrated below this heading on the deepest level, seemed simple enough, but prompted him to investigate the nature of the material involved and its cost. Before long his eyes come to rest on

Assets/Agents and the subtopic, vanadium steel. Drilling down to the second layer, he discovered that it was truly strong and lightweight. So far so good. But again, what about price? On the second level of Pressures to Act, he noted that the competition was pricing their cars at up to $2,000, which gives Ford enormous leeway to compete in the marketplace, as his estimate for the final Model T selling price was only $3–400. But did Ford's project entail any other risks?

As the subject examined Build and Assemble components, he wondered whether workers would continue to work at a job with such an unvarying and unchallenging assembly line, but under Fix Negative Consequences, he saw that Ford believed that if the problem arose, he could rectify it with higher wages and reduced hours. But the red emoticon affixed to Road Test led him to find that Ford's engineers had been worried about the capacity of vanadium steel to support the car's crankshaft. Not good news, but remembering something seen a moment ago, the subject returned to Assets/Agents/vanadium steel and was reminded that vanadium is light and strong. And so, soon after, when he examined the Short-Term Benefits and looked below to learn of a Model T assembly line capable of producing five cars per minute, the subject was sold on the Model T entirely.

PART II

PERSONAL AND GROUP PLANNING

CHAPTER 9

UNCONSCIOUS PERTHINKING AND OTHER AUTOMATIC MENTAL PROCESSES

… in today's world, wherever we turn, talking about the parts and wholes of anything in a consistent and communicable way is becoming increasingly difficult.

INTRODUCTION

The third part of this book concerns itself primarily with the eye's mind and why thinking-by-seeing can be so very idea-friendly. These are not simple matters; they might take some time to grasp satisfactorily, but it's important that you fully appreciate the ways in which visual thinking shapes our decisions, especially when it comes to seeing "meaning-patterns" and extracting critical information from idea-laden structural configurations.

Incidentally, many of the concepts I'll refer to from here on in may strike you as uncomfortably abstract and far too "soft" to apply directly to a world in which hard knocks can follow one after the other time-without-end. If this is indeed the case, let me assure you that these notions are not as theoretical and limp-minded as you might think. Emergence, for example, the process behind the seemingly miraculous appearance of new and often inexplicable animal (and human) behaviors, can't be dismissed as beyond empirical verification or simply irrelevant to our immediate lives and needs.

Many instances of these natural phenomena are happening all around us all the time, such as internet "viral-going" or the ups-and-downs of the stock market. Finally, what makes the idea of emergence so very serviceable is the fact that many of the higher-order thinking processes that might be described as dynamically emergent were once made possible by happenstance environmental and psychological conditions. They are now often made *probable* with the help of "thinking machines" (such as the many mind maps now in circulation and, of course, the U-Template).

BEHIND THE CONFUSION

So, let's start this second half of our journey into the eye's mind with an additional *ad hoc* definition of the U-template: namely, "a tool designed to configure project plans dynamically as well as structurally (part-to-part and part-to whole). Of course, in today's world, wherever we turn, talking about the parts and wholes of *anything* in a consistent and communicable way is becoming increasingly difficult. Just turn on the radio and listen to today's business and political pundits. Do they seem to agree as to "what fits where and how"? If the answer is no, perhaps one reason for this all-out discord is our growing need to "nail down" our current problems one hard nail at a time, expecting, hoping or demanding that the world remain the same as we hammer away at it with our supposedly iron logic.

The notion of a tight-fitting nuts-and-bolts universe, (the cosmos some of us no longer truly believe in), took deep root in our civilization and culture with the writings of the rationalist philosophers, and it wasn't terribly long after, at the dawning of the industrial revolution, that we began to take a machine-like view of virtually everything around us. Alas, most of mankind seems to be stuck with this hard-headed philosophical inheritance, the remnants of our previous millennium's first-this-then-that approach to almost everything we decide to undertake. We continue to support the idea of a fixed-order world that can be managed with the same ease and efficiency that we expect of our household appliances. But as the physicists and social scientists are now telling us, this *Weltanschauung*, this world view, is clearly as faulty and out of date as an old leaking ice box.

But then again, thanks to the new science of complexity,

soft thinking (i.e. seeing things in terms of their dynamic internal interrelationships) has been gaining traction within many of today's academic and technical disciplines. But again, these newer attitudes haven't yet filtered down to the man on the street. He's amenable to these new spooky ideas qua ideas, but he's still slow on the uptake when it comes time to employ them as working models for running his own busy affairs or thinking through his own thoughts.

So, the rigid serial-order mentality continues to dominate our lives. And, I reiterate, if ever there was a world devoid of hard answers to its many soft (shadowy) problems, this mess we find ourselves in is surely it. On September 11, 2001, two very hard airliners flew into two very hard skyscrapers. But the governing variables driving this event, fanaticism and self-renunciation to name just a couple, were ever so soft. In light of the power of soft thinking to upset or restore the world, this writer intends to help empower soft thinking by lending it some hard muscle.[1]

---

1. The term "soft-thinking," as it appears in this book, refers to the tentative recognition of dynamic connections between two or more structural or dynamic elements operating within the same system, i.e., the conceptual linkages we "pencil-in" in order to frame hypotheses and draw conclusions. Unconscious soft thinking—or at least its perceptual aspect—contributes to our sensory-based interpretations of everything that appears before us, natural or man-made. For instance, to be made intelligible, the visual representation of the iron lamppost (into which we might smash our vehicle if we're not careful) must be built up from many of our sensory reactions to its many physical attributes, a mental construction that requires innumerable tabulations, probability assessments, and tail-end guesswork. Furthermore, what we ultimately perceive are not one-to-one readings of these immediate sensory experiences, as the inflowing raw data from the external world never reaches consciousness. So when it comes to thinking about real life and the real world, even the so-called hard facts we learn through experience may not be as rock-solid as we think.

MANEUVERING BETWEEN THE ROCK AND THE HARD PLACE

Why soft, non-linear thinking? A brief thought experiment might provide some of the answers. Imagine you're driving your car along a suburban street. A short distance ahead of you is an open manhole marked off with orange barriers. A little further along, a child is running into the street after a ball. A parked car is about to turn out into the street without any indication of the driver's intention. And now, a truck starts to back into a driveway, and as it swings wide, it appears as though it's going to cut across one of the paths we were about to take to avoid the little girl. The question is … what do *you* do and how do you do it?

Do you asses each situational factor, each possible response, in some meticulously plotted sequence? No, never, because that would take time, and these events are unfolding simultaneously and much too rapidly to "outthink" in the conventional way. What you *do* do is take in the situation as a whole in one hawk-eyed glance, and—as instinctively as a bald eagle in a steep dive—execute a single maneuver with respect to the entire pattern of calamities-in-the-making. You don't even think about it. Your brain has registered the situation in its wholeness and ordered a single coordinated response, in this case a skillful combination of braking and evasive action. In other words, to conceive of things visually is to think of them holistically. And to think of the situation holistically is essentially to be "situationally" on top of it.

Now here's another mental experiment, a close variation of the same scenario based on an equally critical situation. Once again, you're driving your car. But this time, it's mid-winter, and to your consternation, an immense clump of snow has just splattered over your windscreen, reducing your frontal vision by half and prompting you to hit the brakes hard, too hard, sending your vehicle skidding and spinning wildly across the icy road ahead. In the split second available for the right counter-response, you act defensively again, responding with a tricky, unorthodox maneuver via the hand brake. And lo and behold, it works. You're still very much alive and kicking.

So once again the question arises: as the galaxy of conceivable responses flashed through your mind, how did you manage to pick just the right action? As in our first scenario, you hadn't the time to weigh your options one after the other in serial order. So that last-minute epiphany of yours, whence did it come?

Try this for an explanation: Making maximal use of the skimpy visual cues you had to work with, you made a number of inferences that, in effect, filled the blind-spot so that you inferentially "saw" more than what was actually visible through your windscreen. Your response was also informed by sequential flashes of subjective imagery, fleeting visions of several all-too-conceivable futures, (many of them memory-based), that you processed in parallel and, as they say, in "no time at all". You were further instructed by memories of a highly practical nature arising from your backlog of "implicit knowledge," accident-avoidance know-how you had amassed over the years—a bit of motoring savvy you hardly knew you had under your belt until the moment you reacted as you did. So if you were not consciously aware of all this, again, *whence did it come?*

The fact is that we regularly and matter-of-factly gather and process information with the help of an inborn early-warning system whose chief function is the rapid identification of everything and anything that might do us any appreciable harm or good. This animal faculty—the biological consequence of millions of years of evolutionary history—is extraordinarily well-developed, especially when compared to our far more limited symbol-recognition capabilities, the latter a very different set of mental powers that goes back in human history only a few millennia.

As it happens, the human brain has evolved a two-fold response to a world that does not always reveal itself directly and explicitly. Specifically, the visual cortex has developed a number of first-impression and second-impression interpretative capabilities that transform neural impulses flowing inward from the retina into subjective images that are likely to tell us we need to know at that moment in time. This transformative process, the multi-stage reframing of raw sensations into images that ultimately mean something, is what visual thinking, (much of it unconscious), is all about.

Fine. But the eye itself doesn't think, right? No, it doesn't, and unfortunately there's strong scientific disagreement as to the nature of the information-collecting mechanisms behind the visual-thinking process, especially the issue of what we "see" (the information embedded in the subjective image itself) when we think visually. But we do know this: generally speaking, before anything else, we human beings are visual thinkers, learners, and "experiencers" whose minds are capable of seizing and storing an abundance of visual information (nearly half of the mind's capacity is devoted to processing pictorial material) while at the same time our neurological system forms new mental structures that soon tie these images to one another and to images captured in the past.

But the best answer to your question depends in part on what we mean by the term "imagery". In other words, do we really see pictures in our heads? Again, there isn't any unanimously accepted scientific answer to date, but the experts tend to agree that the use of the term "mental imagery" need not imply that bona fide images materialize and linger on in some unspecified region of our brain—in other words, there is no homunculus up there in the balcony watching movies. For instance, there is no denying that champion chess players genuinely "visualize" their moves, but they don't actually entertain mental pictures of wooden or plastic chess pieces moving around the board.

Additionally, the dominance of visual thinking over other sensory mechanisms and experiences varies from individual to individual, and we all have our own ways of thinking and "thinking-in-a-seeing-kind-of-way". Table 1 illustrates the many ways this author ordinarily attends to the world around him. You may recognize some of your own visual-thinking styles somewhere in this list.

So once again, what are these so-called mental images and how do they function down there in the depths of the mind's dark sub-basement? There are many theories bouncing around the psychology labs, but I'll mention just two. The simplest assumption is that that there is little or no difference between the image of the animal with tusks, a long trunk and floppy ears that you might encounter at the zoo, and the image that appears in your mind when you read a book and come across the word "elephant". Other opinions, including those held by champion chess players, have it that we use both image-codes (pictures) and certain verbal-codes (words) to store and retain information, since as common sense would suggest, words that are inherently abstract and/or symbolic are relatively easy to process semantically, whereas words associated with concrete objects are more likely to lend themselves to pictorial interpretations. But as to whether, in theory, we would all be better off using mental imagery exclusively, I'll only say this: no one really doubts that mental imagery tells us more about our day-to-day material world in a shorter time than non-pictorial (symbolic) representations ever can.

Table 1

Sporting events	Watching the event and watching other people watch the event.
Movies	Watching the screen exclusively.
TV	Wandering around the room and attending to things, which I watch as intently as I watch the screen.
Elevators	Staring dumbly up at the numbers.
Circuses	Three rings at the same time.
Nature	Gazing wistfully at everything.
Wall maps and directories	Quickly scanning back and forth.
Paintings	Gazing alternatively between the whole and the parts.
Other people	Taking in quick impressions of their physique, dress, and facial expressions.
City streets	Looking straight through to my destination, unless I'm in Paris.

Compounding the visual-thinking vs. symbolic-thinking issue, it happens that some of us are more frequent—or perhaps more adept—visual-thinkers than others. But although those of us who think in pictures exclusively are in the minority, research has shown that hybrid (part-time) visual-verbal thinkers constitute a good seventy-five percent of the population, and so it's not unreasonable to presume that most of us do our fair share of visual thinking. Furthermore, within the population of visual thinkers, there are significant differences in received pictorial vividness which, when noticeably diminished, seems to affect our ability to detect changes in, and variations among, the images we create as part of our cognitive activity. This may explain why, as they say, there are artists and then there are artists.

Amid the huge fund of widespread expert opinion regarding visual thinking, a popular belief holds that subjective images are more than just pictorial memories lying around passively in our mental storage rooms waiting to be resuscitated on demand. According to this school of thought, imagery should be thought of as an active undertaking, more of a "happening" than a "being", a "does" more than an "is". According to psychologist Steven Pinker, mental imagery is in itself part of an exploratory process, a personal experiment in perception intended to increase our awareness of an outer world yet to be fully comprehended. Pinker is not alone in this belief, for there are other psychologists who are even more purpose-minded, arguing that the mind is continually asking questions, and toward this end it uses images as instruments with which to (literally) measure reality. But no matter what we believe to be the nature of mental imagery, we must admit that this extraordinary "whatsis" comes as close, in its very essence, to a "true" image as anything we might ever imagine.

Having referred to the visual-thinking practices on which chess players tend to rely, I'll now iris in on chess and chess masters for a number of reasons, the first being that in a psychological sense, chess (at least the way grandmasters play it) is quite similar to the standard U-Template routine: both tend to induce a heightened state of situation-awareness, which in turn sparks sharpened situation-specific responses to situations whose initial impact was no more than that of an indistinct information-pattern.

Secondly, in both instances, chess or template, the meaning and/or value of any single piece of the puzzle, (i.e., key word or chess piece) will be determined in part by its current spatial position as well as its semantic/conceptual interrelationships with others of its kind. These values will also be determined (on the chessboard) by rule-bound empowerments/constraints, and (on the U-Template) by personal assessments made on the basis of one's familiarity with the item in question. Both activities require constant shifts of attention between the imperatives of the entire chessboard/template and those imposed by certain critical local conditions.

Case in point: Nikolai Krogius is a Russian chess grandmaster and experienced psychologist whose dual background has led him to certain specific conclusions about chess and its mental mechanics. According to Krogius, the classic "chess image" is not simply an image of the board with its pieces, but instead "an assessment of the typical position in the sense that the image is a generalization which takes into account the peculiar relationships between the pieces and their possible moves".

As Krogius puts it, "the squares and pieces are thus reflected in one's mind not on their own, but as carriers of *the ideas of the position*" (emphasis mine), adding, "the retained image is sometimes caused not by a single piece and its functions or by an individual square on the board, but by a group of pieces or squares with more complex relationships". Finally, "… it is not only individual pieces, squares and moves that remain in the mind in a relatively unchanged form, but also tactical and strategic ideas as well".

Pertti Saariluoma is a cognitive, "content"-oriented psychologist at the University of Helsinki who specializes in the psychology of chess, a popular and fertile area of psychological research these days. Like many experts exploring mental imagery, he is suspicious of the word "seeing" when it is lightly applied to the chess player's canny perceptions. Saariluoma prefers to use the term "apperception," meaning (roughly) a personal thought model containing an admixture of external-world imagery and previously-acquired content-laden knowledge. A fair-enough distinction, since this accent on cognition's contribution to the game is supported by the fact that many expert chess players rarely visualize actual chessboards. Furthermore, as they forage for a promising next move across the board, different players rely on different aspects of what they perceive to be significant. In fact, even the most skillful grandmasters have trouble visualizing every option open to them, and out of the millions of choices to be made, they ordinarily focus on less than a hundred selected attack or defense combinations. It seems that given a certain configuration of pieces on the board, the experienced player seeks out a familiar pattern or "theme of combination" and only then considers the choice of available moves relevant to that particular arrangement. Be that as it may, chess players have little to say about the patterns they choose to follow and how these cues become readily apparent to them during a match, a fair indication that, for the most part, the selection of these themes takes place well below their level of consciousness.

CHAPTER 10

PERSONAL LIFE-CHANGE PLANNING

...but many of my interpretations felt as if they had suddenly come to me from out of nowhere. In other words, they must have crawled into my mind from somewhere deep in my own unconscious.

In my past life in the United States as a psychoanalyst treating a goodly number of Greenwich Village artists and writers, I gradually developed a keen interest in visual imagery and its salutary effects on the human psyche; not only the role it had played in the early lives of my patients, but also, in my own case, the ways in which the power of my own verbal imagery improved and the use of images increasingly crept into my therapeutic commentary. Ultimately, these same mental pictures, mine and theirs, provided me with a foundation upon which I could arrange the thousands of thoughts that not only bore on this or that patient, but also, to a certain degree, on the analyst himself, yours truly. (After all, when you're monitoring the analytic process as it unfolds before your, um, ears, you'd be keeping a close eye on yourself as a major participant in the mix.) During that faraway period of time, practically all of my clinical remarks—and their accompanying ideas and images—were more or less by the book, i.e., pretty much cut and dried. But many of my interpretations felt as if they had suddenly come to me from out of nowhere. In other words, they must have crawled into my mind from somewhere deep within my own unconscious.[1]

As time went on these image-laden observations and conjectures became the basis of my long-term treatment plans, and taken together they provided a framework on which I could pin the thousands of diagnostic estimations I would also have to keep in mind as the treatments progressed. My framework for predicting clinical outcomes included a number of primary improvement criteria, namely, "potential cognitive-emotional gain" (opportuni-

---

1. Let me say this: whenever I was confronted with a new patient, my first order of business was always the same: the establishment of an analytic overview, namely the scoping-out of the job to be done within a quasi-diagnostic framework based on the implicit question, "What's happening here?" Once these initial observations consolidated, I was able to move on to all the subordinate questions related to the patient's inner mental strengths (growth opportunities) and weaknesses (impediments to growth). Once this groundwork was completed, I was in a far better position to guesstimate my patient's chances for a successful treatment and a life altered for the better.

ties), or more abstractly, "dispositional gain" (psychic obstacles gone).

Unfortunately, the complexity of the material I had before me often strained my mental model to the limit, and soon enough the framework I had devised acquired an added dimension as it folded over onto itself into a sandwich-like information-capture system that better accommodated the features of an analysis-in-progress. And so the U-Template was born.

THE UNCONSCIOUS

If by now you're wondering where all this talk of art, imagery and analysis is leading. Well, it's leading to the touchy—and often distracting—subject of the unconscious, that murky netherworld between darkness and light, oblivion and awareness, inadvertence and attention. Although there are those that casually disregard its influence on our lives, others believe that this realm of the mind is so extensive and influential—that the "deeper" mental activities that transpire therein are so vastly responsible for our routine cognitive behavior, i.e., for helping us "get around"—that they boldly assert that consciousness (as we—think—we know it), may be largely superfluous.

Although I have never been a zealous adherent of Sigmund Freud's theories of the unconscious, especially those that speak of a psychic region where motivational demons (Oedipus, Electra, etc.) take control of our thoughts and deeds in our weaker moments, I must state for the record that a number of Freud's ideas pertaining to the existence of involuntary mental processes and their influence on our thoughts and behavior have been well-authenticated time after time in the laboratory. And while many research psychologists disagree as to the extent to which these automatic mechanisms and their susceptibilities control our behavior, the vast majority believe that our most critical mental activities do indeed occur outside of our immediate awareness. Many also believe that these unconscious cerebrations operate along a continuum shared with our more conscious thoughts and that both systems contribute to the processing of sensory-based data into the situation-awareness that gets us safely through the day.

But this public acknowledgement of the mind's two-story structure is nothing new. As we find in most of the world's folk knowledge, there is and has always been a popular belief in a separate "back door" to our awareness of the world at large. For instance, take the term "intuition". For a considerable period of time, we've been applying this label—more correctly than not—to any mental process in which a battery of seemingly non-existent mechanisms deal quickly and effortlessly with incoming patterns of information far too complex to be deciphered methodically.

So quickly and automatically do these unconscious mechanisms tear through their respective chores that psychologists observing human brain activity prior to the execution of certain complex tasks can identify signs of preparatory neural activity well *before* their subjects (willingly) decide to perform them. Further evidence of active non-conscious intent can also be found in the well-documented power of subliminal advertising messages. But although mental processes operating outside of conscious awareness are genuine enough, researchers attempting to locate their origins or determine their specific relationship to our conscious thoughts and feelings have a hard time doing so. It is only by their unmistakable consequences that we can finally distinguish one species of unconscious mental operation from another, or from those that are fully conscious.

Nevertheless, if we could descend deeply enough into the myriad dimensions of human information-processing and have a good look around, we'd find that unconscious processes play a far more pivotal role in these activities than their conscious and easily accessible counterparts. They would be hard at work at their own distinctive tasks, making our many and diverse forms of human sense-making possible. I'm speaking now of the pattern-creation and pattern-recognition faculties that spring into operation whenever the outside world shows us its more equivocal side. As mentioned in the chapter on coherentism, any argument as to the nature of an uncertain state of affairs will seem more reasonable when the pieces of evidence underlying this interpretation support one another within the same meaningful context. It is here, within this matching process, that pattern-recognition (and the cerebral multi-tasking accomplishments that make it possible) ensures that everything that needs sorting out is duly settled, and that the necessary groundwork for further mental processing has been completed satisfactorily.

Put somewhat differently, recognizing that things do or do not fit together has a pivotal role in sparking intuitive breakthroughs. As the psychologist Lois Isenman points out, "Intuitive processing can be understood as analogous to visual perception." Our visual system is unique in this respect, as much of our visual processing occurs in parallel inside the eye's mind, which finally acts on—only—that which it deems to be most important.

In the course of a normal day, we are kept informed of the world around us by "eyefuls" of particulars that bombard us every waking hour of the day, a vast barrage of information that is quickly worked over by mental machines that trim it all down to an assortment of cues as to what needs to be done next. The operative word is relevance, and this is what the eye's mind looks for as it jumps object to object throughout our range of vision.

Here's an example. Let's say we happen to notice our dog Rover out of the corner of our eye. He's pacing back and forth across the floor and wagging his tail to emphasize his desperate need for a short walk and an opportunity to relieve himself against a nearby tree. Right behind this scene of canine discomfort, as seen through a large picture window, the weather outside is sunny and mild. Finally, our eyes alight on the chair on which Rover's favorite leash dangles. Yes, it might be a good idea to walk him right away. Ahh! Great idea!! Let's do it.

This, then, was the essence of our visual behavior at the time. Except for a few fleeting images of other things to which we might have payed brief attention at that moment, nothing else occupied our minds. At least not our conscious minds. The other, more unconscious part of our mind had been busy all this time tending to its own chores and making its own observations. It noticed a number of things consciousness did not, and had already stored away these "irrelevant" impressions (e.g., a stranger entering a neighbor's house) for future reference at a time when some mental association, (e.g., hearing the house was burgled at that moment), might finally drag the memory into the light of day.

To sum up, we are all capable of doing many things at once, thanks to integrative mental mechanisms operating in realms far below consciousness. This parallel-processing faculty is just one part of our neural intake-output system, whose task is to coordinate environmental and/ or bodily signals and their more significant interactions.

**HOLISTICS AND GESTALTS: WHEN THE UNCONSCIOUS MIND
GETS IT WRONG TO GET IT RIGHT**

Take a look at the illustration above. Do you see a panda, or do you see seven black shapes? Do you see a figure, or do you see a number of parts? If you see a whole panda, it's because your unconscious mind is conning you into seeing a "Gestalt" (a whole), the product of the brain's self-organizing and unifying function. Following the law of prägnanz (good form), we tend to react to incomplete images by filling in the gaps and eliminating the extraneous. If you have any doubts about this "perfect-making" process and its influence on our everyday perceptions, take a look at (1) this visually assisted closure of an incomplete circle, and (2) the figure-ground ambiguity shown here.

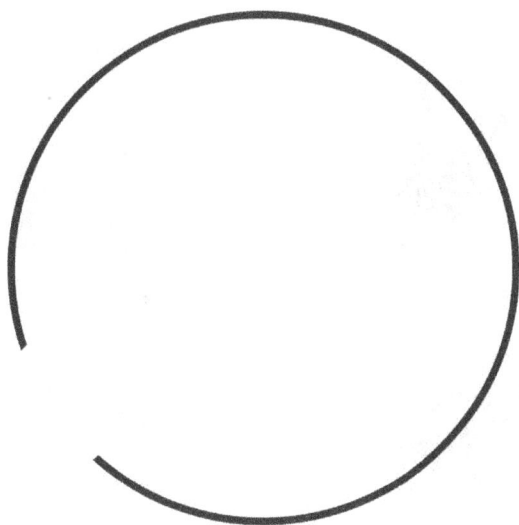

Incomplete circle (1)

These illustrations reveal so very convincingly that our immediate sense of what is real is the end-product of an unconscious decision-making process, a kind of visual conclusion we reach when things seem whole enough to identify as recognized objects.

Of course, as the bi-stable illustrations (2), (3) demonstrate, (the two-fold perception can come to rest in either of two states), there are times when what is real to us is really *up* to us. When we come upon two adjacent configurations are that are evenly recognizable and the eye per-

Figure/ground ambiguity (2)

Bi-stable illustration (3)

ceives one of them, we can reverse this behavior at will. (Go ahead and try it. I'll wait.)

For almost a hundred years, Gestalt psychologists have familiarized us with many of these so-called optical illusions, suggesting that there are many ways in which our unconscious perceptual apparatus helps us to see wholes, sometimes for the better, sometimes not (e.g., "seeing" channels on the surface of Mars was not helpful to anyone but science-fiction writers). And by playing these tricks on our eye's mind so very effectively, perceptual ambiguities force us to appreciate how, on certain occasions, unconscious self-deception can help us navigate our private worlds in accordance with what we only choose to see.

The Gestalt advantage becomes strikingly apparent when we think about the things that we perceive as constant and uninterrupted–even when they may not be so very "regular" at all. For example, when our view of a (familiar) physical object happens to be partially obstructed and one or more of its component parts are thereupon lost from view, we tend to fill in the gap by reconstructing the absent segments in our imagination. Think of the about-to-be-sawed-in-half magician's assistant: all we need to see is her head and two feet to get us shuddering at the fate awaiting the body part that's out of sight.

But should we be terribly surprised to find that "whole-making" is one of our more expedient self-deceptions? Our humanoid ancestors were creatures often forced by ecological changes to leave their trees and, on only two legs, prowl the open savannah for their daily victuals, a risky business that required a sharp eye for four-legged predators often prowling the neighborhood more than one sabre-tooth tiger at a time. What we needed and what we got was a hair-trigger warning system (such as a heightened sensitivity to pattern-based images and fig-ure-ground differences) to facilitate our escape to safety with only those two flimsy legs under us to get us there in timely fashion.

So once again, what are we referring to when we speak of wholes? In plain language, wholes are the psychological building blocks we use to form coherent and intelligible pictures of the world we live in. Progressing upward in the hierarchy of whole forms we find the subatomic, the atomic, the molecular, the chemical, the physical, the biological and yes, the psychological (e.g., that catchy tune you can't stop humming).[2]

As an intrinsic property of all things real and imaginary, wholeness might be described as both a state of being and a state of mind. As a conclusive perception, it reflects the unconscious mind's ability to interpret endless streams of information along with the complex part-to-part inter-relationships responsible for their perceptual coherence. So, for the sake of convenience, let's just say that whole-ness, in the psychological sense, is the power of the eye's mind to "see the whole picture", "the big Kahuna". So indispensable is our holistic perspective that without it, we might never be able to absorb the endless bits of visual, auditory, and kinetic stimuli that relentlessly impinge on our sense organs. Without our mind's uncon-scious whole-making ability, these pointillist signals from the world around us would defy our best efforts to under-

2. The basis of a melody's "catchy-ness" is not only in the music we hear as we hum it, but also our tacit acknowledgement of where the tune is heading. Take it from an experienced songwriter: the extremely repetitive, single note introduction ("Like the beat, beat, beat," etc., up to the "Night and ..." of Cole Porter's "Night and Day") is so very compelling because we've previ-ously internalized the song *as a whole*, and as we hum these first words of the verse we're already anticipating the gorgeous harmonic surge that begins with the third word of the chorus, ("day-y-y-y").

stand anything at all about what's going on out there in the world of the visibly whole.

TWICE THE VISION FOR THE PRICE OF ONE

You may have had the occasion to tell an acquaintance something like this: "I stopped dead in my tracks, but I didn't know why ... until I realized after a while that the person I was staring at had to be you. Did you do something with your hair?"

That this sort of event is not at all that uncommon tells us heaps about the frequency and import of unconscious object recognition. As previously mentioned, when something appears suddenly before our eyes, its immediate impingement on the retina ordinarily elicits a pre-conscious, pre-recognition cerebral response. ("Spots!! A leopard??") This first impression, partial and selective, shows us but doesn't quite tell us what we're looking at, as our built-in identification devices often trade off specificity-of-perceived-detail for speed-of-response. In an instant we—pre-consciously—recognize, at best, size, shape, orientation, direction, and position before a second visual engine kicks in, enabling us to decipher whatever's left of the available visual information and decide whether we want to explore it further. But during the first stage of the experience our visio-spatial apparatus has quite enough to work with, so that if necessary, it can warn us immediately to fight or take flight—or tarry if we spy something out there resembling dinner. This first half of our perceptual response consumes so little of our time that the target object's remaining features can be subsequently processed far more carefully than otherwise; that is, the more information the first image conveys, such as "there's nothing suspicious going on out there", the greater the opportunity to take a better look around for other environmental cues as what to do next. And since our attention mechanisms can also scan the second, richer image for a more detailed view of the object of interest, the less we find to worry us, the easier and quicker we can go on about the business of surviving.[3]

I bring this matter of to your attention not only because it illustrates the immense practical value of thinking visually, but because it reminds us that if this two-phase description of the visual process were to apply not only to images originating in the environment but also to those ideas we initially "see" (dream up in the form of images), then it follows that before we set out to develop an idea, it might be wise to spend a moment or two deciding whether or not to put our thoughts on paper as they "hit us" or, alternatively, to work things out only after we believe that we've absorbed their full impact (the U-Template is all about the former process).

If the matters we've just explored are somewhat fuzzy and conjectural here and there, the following piece of news (likewise bearing on the decoding of sensory material, but now as it applies to our own ideas when they are made—literally—visible) is well-tested: it's about what happens once we decide to put things down on paper. The news coming out of the psychology laboratories is that even when ideas expressed graphically—e.g., illustrations,

3. Now here you might want to ask *a propos* of the U-Template: Does this two-stage visual process occur in the presence of written symbols, words in particular? In answer, it's beyond this author's knowledge, but it's quite possible. Whether we perceive things twice—in the larger sense--when we peer at these word patterns remains unclear, but there is no reason to assume that the same rules don't apply. Perhaps when we scan words "naively", as we do when perusing a U-Template, we get two separate opportunities to interpret them.

maps—have been consummately rendered, they will nevertheless appear to be somewhat dissimilar to the initial—subjective—images they were intended to capture. This disparity—between original and "copy"—will tell us something new and, if we're lucky, highly revealing, as the two different versions will augment each other in ways we might not have anticipated. Creating a certain "surplus value".

VIDEO INTRODUCTION TO THE PERSONAL U-TEMPLATE

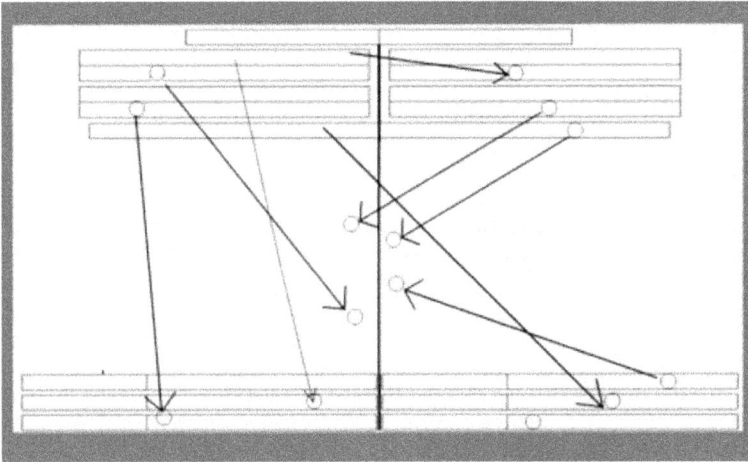

For a simple video introduction to the U-Template personal planning process, go to u-template.com

CHAPTER 11

PERSONAL PLANNING: WHEN IT'S STICKY BUSINESS, STICK TO THE BASICS

The personal plan takes on the equivalence of a standard psychological test

t's time now to move on from the unconscious mechanisms we've just now covered and touch down on a much broader topic: the mental mechanics, conscious and unconscious, of the personal planning process. As there are so many ways in which the benefits of personal planning correspond with the corporate planning matters we've explored in earlier chapters, there's no need to plough through this nearly identical material a second time. But there's certainly new territory to be explored, much of it motivational in nature; for this new subject—and here we're talking largely about planning on a life-changing scale—contains matters of great interest all its own, and any discussion of personal planning must include some detailed description of mental "bootstrapping" and other psychologically self-transformative processes. Certainly any review of the nature and dynamics of life-change planning must take into account the unconscious mechanisms responsible for personal planning-derived benefits. And therefore the business of initializing a life change—self-motivated or otherwise—merits an enquiry of its own.

LIFE-CHANGE PLANNING

It goes without saying that a life project (and a self-driven life change is almost always a major project) is by definition a big-picture affair. It can be a desperate, get-through-it-alive stratagem or, on the other side of the spectrum, one of those "self-realizing" years-long affairs we saw so much of in the late sixties and early seventies. These extended exercises in self-transformation, often rooted in monumental commitments to one's own future, proved to be quite successful in their own way, but also so very costly—with payouts to psychologists, gurus, etc. Indeed, it often seemed to this ex-practitioner that more than a few of his long-term patients were treating their future lives with a regard bordering on reverence, as if they were poring over a rare manuscript, all the while preserving a certain distance between their thoughts and the living, breathing selves that would soon inhabit the new lives they were preparing for. But in those far more opportune mid-century decades, people seemed to have a clearer idea, sensible or not, of who it was they wanted to be and what it was they wanted to accomplish when they finally got there.

Insofar as there is no doubt that motivational factors heavily influence the personal planning process, we will now turn to some recent scientific research on human self-incentivizing and in particular, a most interesting scientific finding: that the "future-gazing" aspect of the personal planning experience can, by and of itself, act as a motivational self-starter. In fact, as recent research has demonstrated, each time we sit down with a pen and paper (or laptop) to formulate a life-changing plan, a mere glimpse of ourselves, subjective or objective, (i.e. of the new and better "me", now fully capable of building better life), can transform what were once merely pipe dreams into new and powerful intentions and undertakings. So, if you'll allow me to address this subject as substantively as it deserves, I'll try to talk you through it in a manner that befits its curious—and perhaps inspirational—implications.

First, as an introduction to this topic, a bit of off-the-cuff advice to those who are already thinking of testing or refining their next personal plan on a U-Template. Whereas your typical corporate plan—excluding its own thorny human-nature issues—ordinarily focuses on large numbers of concrete and quantifiable variables, its operational guidelines will not apply—entirely and in the same way—to the problems addressed and dealt with in most personal plans. As a general rule, given their relatively limited variety of rock-bottom concerns, (self-esteem, relationships, finances, etc.,) and solutions (e.g., psy-chotherapy, self-improvement, job-training), the formu-lation and implementation of the personal plan, although just as "iffy" as its business counterpart, tends to be rela-tively straightforward.[1]

Another difference: personal plans, often found to be awash in preference-based issues reflecting a hodgepodge of human needs and satisfactions, are, in this author's opinion, best conceived and outlined in bold strokes, one problematic layer at a time. Think of the way you might fill the pages of a photo album, arranging your snapshots in patterns that are meaningful primarily on an intuitive level: that is, relative to a miscellany of time frames, loca-tions, friends and so on, as if the pages themselves were establishing their own primal framework.

Finally, having put personal planning in some sort of gen-eral perspective, it's time to think once again—but quite differently—about visual thinking and planning on a psy-chological level, and especially, this time around, what goes on in our heads when we attempt to look into the future for the express purpose of making a dramatic life-change. We'll now examine some of the reasons why per-sonal plans, apart from their expository benefits, (they show us what needs to be done, to what extent, and in what order), can be so very behaviorally compelling ... lit-erally so. We'll also try to determine whether, as many psychologists claim, simply seeing into one's own future can transform mere expectation into factual reality, for

---

1. I mean this in the practical sense only. On the private stage, there are likely to be relatively fewer available scenarios and just a few actors (e.g., relatives and friends) to help play them out, which is to suggest that for most of us, given our few resources and options, we can address only so many chal-lenges in a lifetime.

there's no doubt that the images and thoughts we conjure up as we formulate our plans do seem to have a will and influence of their own. Accordingly, if they can spur us on as effectively as they seem to do, then under the right conditions, these "visions" can make the personal planning exercise and its aftermath prove to be far less arduous and stressful than one might anticipate.

Now to work. Let's embark on our examination of life-change personal planning by underlining the obvious: most of us make plans such as these in order to anticipate the things we must do to insure the successful completion of what may conceivably prove to be monumental enterprise. But aside from its preparatory advantages, personal planning can be helpful in an altogether different manner: if the plan under review is sufficiently detailed and at least seemingly appropriate, it can validate our aspirations by providing us with a special mirror with which to assess the state of mind of the plan's primary author (i.e., ourselves). It tells us not only where we want to go and how to get there ... but who we are. Right now. It is in this capacity that the personal plan takes on the equivalence of a standard psychological test, reflecting back to us a picture of ourselves and our deepest feelings about our lives: past, present and (hypothetical) future.[2]

In other words, just as form tends to follow function, the

2. It goes without saying that in order to put together a life-changing plan we are truly equipped to follow, we should first consider our personal capabilities and whether or not they can support us in the rather formidable task of altering the future. Not that we must draft our plans with the tactical precision of a corporation developing a new product. No, a personal plan is more like a completed picture puzzle than a quasi-military strategy. One only need make certain that the pieces fit together neatly without having to be squeezed out of shape to do so (which will prove to be no small task without the help of the right planning tool).

overall form of our personal plans and the life-changes they anticipate should stem inescapably in accordance with, or perhaps in defiance of, the lives we've been living all along. At the end of the day, plans should reflect the human needs they're designed to serve, which tells us that before we make plans and commit to them, we'd better keep in mind who we are, who we have been, and given the odds for or against us, what kind of person we might prove to be by the time we get where we want to go. It follows then that if our plan is suspiciously effortless, inordinately difficult, or skewed in some unusual direction, we must ask ourselves before anything else, "Is this plan really me?"

PERSONAL PLANNING, GOAL-SETTING, AND THE
UNCONSCIOUS

... our intentions can change us. It's as if in a moment of high purpose we dangle a carrot before our eyes' mind as an inducement to get moving and do what needs to be done.

Now to a few themes bearing on personal planning's psychological underpinnings and some recent scientific findings with respect to personal future-gazing, a process—often the simple act of watching the "road ahead"—that has the power to transform us well beyond our personal expectations, no matter if the "eyeful" that motivates and finally modifies us is real or illusory. An exaggeration? Maybe. But not so far from the truth, so help me. Indeed, under certain circumstances we can achieve these benefits by simply imagining our personal changes—i.e., the "truth" doesn't always matter as long as the conditions are right. Sounds a bit like pie in the sky? Well, read on – the magic word is "feedforward," and we'll get to it in just a moment.

But first the back-story, namely goal-setting and its benefits. It goes as follows: once we "see"—and we needn't literally *see*—ourselves performing more effectively than we have in the past, this experience, alone, (envisioning the future improvement and/or the path we must take to achieve it) will spur us on to live up to its example. It's all about intention, motivational "boot-strapping," and the benefits of "self-efficacy".

Albert Bandura, one of the giants of research psychology, has demonstrated fully and conclusively that, in his own words, "people are proactive, aspiring organisms". Translated, we are not only self-directing but ... how can I put it? Well ... self-*propelling*. He and his colleagues have established that to be proficient at a task, a sufficient sense of self-efficacy, a (realistic) "I can do that" response to a specific challenge, can be of major importance. In other words, if we're to rise to the occasion, we must believe that we're capable of doing so (followed by a strong personal commitment to the task lying before us).

In essence, Bandura's theoretical model rests on the notion that forethought can act as a self-energizing and self-directing motivator. Unlike the aforementioned feedforward process (yet to be unveiled), self-efficacy-driven positive change requires the investment of substantial time and effort on our part. We must set goals and pursue them in accordance with (1) our environmental circumstances and personal standards, (2) our newly formed "outcome expectancies", and (3) our willingness to self-monitor the behavior called for by the task.

Bandura's model, as reasonable (and probably familiar) as it may seem, raises some intriguing questions regarding behavioral feedback and, in many instances, the actual (paradoxical) moment of its (unlikely) psychological impact. As is widely known, your standard feedback process is a simple three-stage affair, at least on the face of it, involving: (1) action (you do something), (2) information (you learn how well you've done it), and (3) subsequent action (you do the same thing better, worse, or merely differently, depending on the nature of the feedback and the manner in which you directly respond to it). Keep in mind that in the course of the classic feedback process, according to its classic definition, *first* comes the initial effort and *then* comes the all-important "results", sent back to us hot off the press, as it were.[3]

---

3. At the end of the day the feedback-as-learning-experience is only the old "hot stove" effect by another name, which, if you stop to think about it (especially if you've ever burned a finger yourself), boils down conceptually to the familiar trial-and-error learning process, especially if we keep in mind that previously-established feedback loops can dampen or amplify the learning process for better or worse. For instance, if the feedback is tied to personal "masochistic" tendencies with power corrupting everything we might ever learn, soon enough we're likely to scorch still another finger, perhaps even the same way we did the last time.

All in all, the feedback response is a cardinal fact of our workaday lives; shaping, re-shaping, or simply sustaining our behavior one action-response-action cycle at a time. But as previously suggested, there's at least one learning environment in which the feedback process seems to work … backwards. In one of the most complex and somewhat unaccountable examples of what seems to be a cognitive process in reverse, the human goal-setting procedure (powered by Bandura's "self-efficacy") appears to improve our chances of success at the very moment we set the goal, well before the specified goal-achieving behavior gets underway, and certainly well before any recognizable positive alteration of our personal circumstances and its corresponding positive feedback. It's a transformation produced by that future-looking some-thing-or-other (a simple cognitive structure/dynamic, it would seem) which goal-setting theorists refer to as "intentionality". Yes, our intentions can change us. It's as if in a moment of high purpose. we dangle a carrot before our eyes' mind as an inducement to get moving and do what needs to be done. (But the clear advantage of goal-setting is such a familiar one that I'm sure we can now part from this topic without losing a single thread of the story.)

Now back to the issue of feedforward and this time to those research psychologists who study the phenomenon under conditions they describe as "video self-modelling". As one of the most vivid and irrefutable examples of feed-back-in-*reverse*, this personal motivator/enabler would appear to be a psychological second cousin to the tra-ditional goal-setting procedure. But as I've already sug-gested, under feedforward conditions we—i.e., their clin-ical subjects—don't (actively) set goals at all, much less try hard, if at all, to achieve them. In fact, we don't appear to need to do anything but just ... watch. Here, as in your classical goal-setting procedure, the future undoubtedly influences the past, but this time, it all reaches a new level of jaw-dropping incredulity.

In a typical experimental setting, subjects known for their behavioral deficiencies/derelictions are exposed to video images doctored (spliced, rearranged) in such a way that they, the subjects, are convinced that there, on the monitor, they are successfully performing tasks... they simply *can't do*. Like Woody Allen on the gallows, his life flashing before his eyes (but, unfortunately, it's someone else's life), video-watching self-modelers are hoodwinked by what they see of "themselves". In these special circumstances they're conned into a state of honest-to-god competence and soon perform quite up to scratch: there's been no effort to exceed themselves, no earned reward, no correct feedback, nothing but the flimflam video tape. How can this be, one wonders? Well, just read the journals. They demonstrate without question that if we are led to (literally) see ourselves as models of competence, then, eventually, *we become that model*.

I should also add that these laboratory-grown improvements, as reported, are even more significant than we might imagine. In the classic self-efficacy-driven goal-setting process, improvement progresses gradually over a goodly period of time (the improvement displayed ordinarily requires multiple trials and continual post-performance feedback), but the improved performance via the feedforward video feedback is a pre-performance process, and the treatment seems to "take" during or soon after the period of time in which the deceptive image flickers on the screen.

To reiterate: although the feedback loop ordinarily does a decent job of shaping our behavior over an extended time period, (by informing us, trial after trial, whether or not—and if so. how much—we've succeeded at a particular undertaking), the feedforward experience via video self-modelling does the job in a flash and through out-and-out deception. So, once again, how can it be that, in this set of circumstances at least, the future can inform the past? Isn't the whole business ass-backwards, a teleological impossibility? The answer is … I really don't know. But I do know one thing for sure, that what awaits us somewhere in the future, real or imaginary, can change our lives smack in the living present. So compelling is the pull-forward of feedforward that once we've been caught in its powerful grip, we can do things that we never dreamed possible. Well, maybe not under all conditions. But as a general rule, if we can create the future in the psychological here and now, we're already halfway there. Sounds a little like the U-Template's personal-planning process? U betcha.

PART III

FINAL THOUGHTS

CHAPTER 12

A SYSTEMS THINKING PRIMER

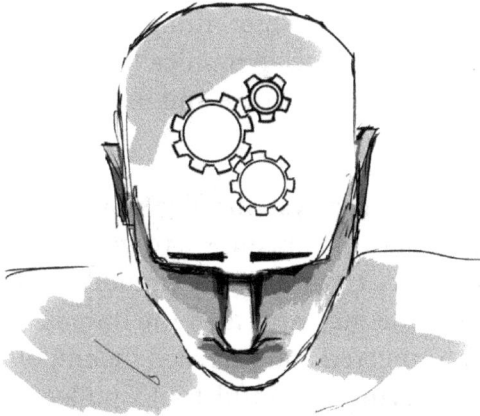

The interrelationships among the parts of a system, any system, may be one-to-one, one-to several, and several-to-several. Furthermore, these established linkages may serve one or more dynamic purposes, namely amplifying, damping internal processes, or, if you've struck gold, "emergence-making".

Throughout this book we've been concentrating on holistic visualization and the wholesale interpretation of complex patterns of information. However, if we were to rely on these concepts (and *only* these concepts) to describe the ways in which our eye's mind decodes the world we live in, we would surely be caught short, as they would suffice only in a world frozen in time, a world with no past, present and future, a world no longer "alive." But the world is hardly static: it is forever diversifying and evolving, and if it were necessary to limit our frame of reference to holistics alone, we'd have to narrow our focus to the thinnest sliver of time. And when all would be said and done, we still wouldn't understand the way things "work".

Welcome to the real world, a world characterized by unremitting action and activity, where things change, and these changes change other things, and where all such changes are driven by dynamically interrelated forces that are system-like in nature and in their influence upon one another.

But what exactly is a system? The notion of systems and systems dynamics has been borrowed heavily from the biological sciences, where early in medical history it was observed that the many parts of the human body are very much interconnected and interdependent, often to a critical degree. Having a painful tooth pulled or a diseased appendix removed will ordinarily do no damage to your biological system, but I wouldn't recommend that you have your cerebral cortex excised without the advice of your family physician.

Systems are characteristically composed of elements that act together, interdependently or not, and the nature and extent of this interaction finally determines the system's complexity and ultimate manageability. The greater the complexity, the smaller the impact each contributing part will have on the whole. Systems tend to be recursive: they might accommodate entire sub-systems, and these sub-systems their own sub-systems, and so on.[1] Always, however, a system's characteristics, in toto, will have a significant influence on its ultimate behavior; enlarging, diminishing or altering certain operations over time as dictated by the prevailing internal and external conditions (its current system state and/or the external environment). It's no surprise then that systems thinking, as it's known, can prove to be a demanding undertaking for those who, for any number of reasons, might seek to get to a system's "beating heart" and make critical changes.

Of course, systems, as we know them are only man-made abstractions, handy constructs if you will, and any system that we might happen to come across in the course of an extended project analysis will exist (as a recognized system) merely in the eye of the beholder. In other words, the questions surrounding the existence of specific systems are partly psychological in nature and ordinarily depend on the nature of their internal organization and/or operations *as we perceive them.* Just try to find the "system" in that old adage, "you can't beat the system".[2]

1. An automobile's fully dependent elements (e.g., the engine, the driver) require each other's integrated contribution to the auto's performance, while its decidedly independent elements, e.g., the rear-view mirror or the coat of paint, do not. Of course, the influence of the automobile's functional interdependencies can be formidable: this "soft stuff", linkages that can extend across entire networks of automotive parts and functions, will ordinarily outnumber the elements themselves, connecting them in ways we may not appreciate until they inexplicably change or disappear.

2. For the moment, let's define systems as broadly as possible, as an organized scheme of things whose interconnected parts operate together as a unified entity (and do so even while interacting with other unified systems). Systems consume inputs and produce outputs regulated by their own internal control guides. The American political system is a set of organized principles, rules, and departments. Its internal mechanisms are powered and maintained by a number of national, state, city, and local entities, at least two political parties, the tripartite executive-judicial-legislative system, and,

There are systems and then there are Systems (of a "higher order"). According to management expert Peter Senge, systems often teem with properties that are merely latent and have not yet materialized into observable structures or behaviors; but given the right conditions, they somehow exhibit unexpected and often startling characteristics. These "gifts from God"—the beauty of the flocking behavior of birds is one striking example—seem to appear before us whole and intact, and are referred to by behavioral, cognitive, and social scientists as "emergent" characteristics.

This notion of emergence might very well apply to the "system" you yourself might be constructing at this very moment, let's say ... a new and novel project-worthy idea (and yes, ideas that "accept input and provide output" can be thought of as systems). Indeed, this brainstorm of yours might have occurred to you just recently and so, still in its embryonic stage, it lies there partially out of sight and mind, waiting to emerge at the first opportunity, lights flashing and bells ringing.[3]

Of course, emergent events aren't always happy ones, but when they are, they can heighten the worthiness of vir-

equally supporting and constraining all this, a written constitution. Historically, this system and its numerous sub-systems have performed more-or-less adequately, sometimes magnificently, but due to its enormous complexity, any discordant event within the system can quickly trigger a sudden collapse, in this instance a tsunami of political, economic, or social upheavals (e.g., consider the 1929 stock market crash or the civil war draft riots).

3. This leads this writer to believe that if this planet of ours, a seemingly limitless hierarchy of wholes and systems, is some kind of miracle-making machine, then as denizens in this ever-changing world, we should be able to act in concert with its ever-unfolding processes, and bring forth our own marvels of human creation.

tually everything around them. Think of the emergence of the Ford Model T and its equally emergent features: a lightweight body, an easy fix-it-yourself parts supply and a high gas mileage, innovations that greatly enhanced our quality of life quite apart from their recognizable impact on our daily transportation habits. Soon after Ford's new "friendly" car arrived on our streets, civilization gradually reorganized itself around the Motoring Style, and before long our day-to-day lives (and dreams) had changed radically. In fact, a social and cultural transformation took place across America, as exemplified in our historic migration from large cities to their adjoining suburbs. And as cars became more widely available and women took advantage of their new freedom of mobility, they also took on new roles, which in turn led to their elevated status in society and the added satisfaction of far more extensive women's rights and privileges.

Whether he knew it or not at the time, Ford had struck gold when he used the notion of "friendliness" as a touchstone for the imminent development of his new car, the consequence of bright idea that soon evolved into something quite extraordinary and unexpected; a new worldwide psychological reality in which we seemed to fuse mentally and corporally with the cars we were droving morning noon and night. One might go as far to say that the automobile had become a metaphoric extension of our bodies and minds, that its fledgling drivers had suddenly acquired an entirely new set of limbs along with the certainty that with just the turn of an ignition key and a stomp of a foot on the gas pedal they could be somewhere else. Anyone who has ever driven a car should remember their first time behind the wheel and the exhilarating experience of near-godliness: of personal transcendence far beyond the satisfactions of car-ownership and ease of travel. It was almost as if one could simply imagine one's destination, and then—within a short period of time spent behind the wheel, voila, there you are. Or there. Or there. Omnipresence for the common man. How emergent can you get?

CHAPTER 13

RANDOM THOUGHTS ON EXPRESSING DOUBT OR, 'WHY EMOTICONS?'

"If a man will begin with certainties, he shall end in doubts; but if he will be content to begin with doubts, he shall end in certainties." — *Francis Bacon*

M any years ago, I came upon a short story that, as the saying goes, "changed my life forever". I can't remember who wrote it, but I believe it was titled *Gulliver*, and the story went as follows:

> *A man takes a quiet stroll in the park, falls into a faint and wakes up soon after, dazed and confused, in an uncomfortably low-ceilinged cell furnished with what appears to be items taken from a child's playroom, whereupon a group of visitors, dwarfed by Gulliver's towering size, invade his room and taunt him about his gigantism. Gulliver is mortified and seemingly defeated. But as the narrative reaches its climax, Gulliver realizes (yes, you guessed it) that the visitors, not Gulliver, were the "freaks", former circus sideshow performers embittered by the ridicule they faced in the course of their carnival careers. Gulliver as laughing-stock was to be their final revenge on mankind.*

The story of Gulliver sticks in my memory for a number of reasons, but what I remember most clearly is its breathtaking turning point, where our Gulliver, wracked by anxiety and confusion but also sensing "something funny going on" seizes a nearby object recently flung his way by his tormenters and lets it drop again, this time carefully noting the time it takes to reach the floor. Case solved. The truth will out.

An improbable feat, but Gulliver's reality test fills me with wonder to this day. (In fact, a readiness to respond to strange emanations in the air—something *wrong* in the room—became one of the keys to my personal psycho-analytic technique. Its cardinal rule: when in the slightest doubt, doubt *everything*.)

I tell the tale of Gulliver because in this age of the unlikely—yet there it is at every turn—"Black Swan", Gulliver's woeful turn-of-fortune could easily be ours. And if anything can happen ... well, you know Murphy's Law. So perhaps the moral of Gulliver's tale is to remain alert for the anomalous, the unexpected, the un-"fit".

By the way, ever hear someone (yourself, maybe?) go on and on about something or other with an air of biblical conviction ... until, with a shrug and a sheepish, "but what do I know" they give the game (their aura of certainty) away? Play the fool or not, we all have a perfect right to parade our ideas before the world like proud mother hens—despite the uninvited duck squawking jauntily at the end of the line—even if the ideas that issue from our mind "have issues", e.g., loose ends to be accounted for. Assigning qualifiers (such as cautionary emoticons) to point out our uncertainties will do nicely in these instances. So, the next time you submit an idea to a U-Template review by your peers, don't hesitate to draw attention its more "iffy" features—using one of your emoticons to sound the proper alert.

A SHORT DISQUISITION ON DOUBT ITSELF

When circumstances compel us to question our own intellectual handiwork, the doubts they raise are likely to appear in many shapes and sizes: such as (a) doubts as to the soundness of this, our latest brainchild, or (b) doubts as to whether or not we are right to doubt the item, and (c), (d) and (e to infinity), doubts, free-floating and spooky, that can continue to haunt us world without end regarding (a) and (b) especially if we're the doubting type.

But aside from these chafing reminders of our own imperfections, (the dogged "nagging-ness" of those doubts that speak not their name), does it matter in the end how or why we harbor these misgivings? In the long run, do these matters—of origin and type—matter?

The question of doubt, its nature and significance, has been hashed over by serious thinkers ever since man invented the Positive Statement, and so we should be careful to pay this most delicate of cognitive dispositions the respect it deserves, even if only with a brief remark or two on the subject. To this end, let's start with a few dictionary definitions of the ill-famed "d" word. In no particular order, they are:—

1. A status between belief and disbelief involving uncertainty or distrust or lack of sureness
2. A feeling of uncertainty or lack of conviction
3. To believe that something may not be true or is unlikely
4. To have no confidence in someone or something.
5. A state of both affirmation and denial

Now let's keep these definitions in mind while we have a look at some of the issues that often arise when we're struggling to overcome our doubts about, for instance, the third stage of our latest plan. Let's assume that we can't quite decide whether the wobbly feeling that comes upon us when we think deeply about the matter concerns our Stage Three scenario (directly) or, as mentioned earlier, it (indirectly) concerns our competence to cast these doubts legitimately in the first place.

To see how significant these questions can prove to be in daily life, let's agree for the moment that the greater one's confidence in a proposition, the more likely one is to believe in its soundness and power to stand up under criticism—and thus its openness to investigation. Which means that if we happen to question the validity of an idea we've just hatched, we're apt to poke cheerfully around in its innards to locate the source of any problems we might suspect are lurking beneath the surface and perform major surgery—a conceptectomy— if necessary. If our efforts fail, we can always abandon the procedure (and the patient) and turn our attention to something more promising.

But where there is *self*-doubt—as to one's ability to "do the surgery", and by implication, to do have done the original "brain-work" properly—this residual ambiguity is unlikely to prompt one to do very much about *anything*. Of course, no matter how we happen to doubt, whether it concerns one's creations or one's capabilities, any such misgiving may in fact be entirely misplaced. In these instances, we also lose out. Where it's the founding idea that we (mistakenly) happen to question, we may then find ourselves squandering precious time in pursuit of that—needless—something-else. And if the former applies, (if the insecurity involves *us*), we would be just as wrongheaded (and twice as self-defeating) to sit on our hands and do nothing of any consequence for as long as it takes us to recover our peace of mind. The moral of this story? When doubt reaches a critical level, the best way out may well be the easiest. (Simply to turn the problem over to someone else). And do it with the help of one of the U-Template's four emoticons.

CHAPTER 14

FOR BUSINESS AND
INSTITUTIONAL READERS

**WHY THE U-TEMPLATE SHOULD BE AN INTEGRAL PART OF
YOUR ORGANIZATION'S PROJECT MANAGEMENT
CAPABILITIES**

t's hardly startling news that in these hectic times,
businesses must adapt as quickly as possible to rapidly
changing environmental conditions, and that their
eventual success will hinge on their ability to bring
together people, processes, technologies, and policies in

ways that enhance the organization's competitive capabilities. Until now, project managers have had to juggle widely varying planning, execution, and control formats along with an equally wide variety of project plan structures and contents, rendering most collaboration between team members and other stakeholders far less effective than they might have been under more uniform conditions.

In the past, there was no standardized procedure for gathering and disseminating project requirements, and this limitation made things inordinately difficult for collaborators who were compelled to fall back on tools and techniques—narrow and often inscrutable batteries of independent analytic instruments—that failed to accommodate the myriads of communication styles that colored their thinking and planning. Moreover, when project managers had to gather and document collaborator expertise, the report did not always fit within an applicable context that could be easily shared with others and serve as a repository for further information of the same nature. As projects develop over time, collaborators require methods and/or mechanisms that allow them to tap into the organization's available stockpile of knowledge. Finally, experts drafted into a project-support role tended to be most focused on the problems and issues associated with their own conceptual frameworks and tended to gravitate toward those project issues with which they were most familiar.

This technical insularity and narrow-band data generation still presents a major impediment to project development, especially on the conceptual side, e.g., where collaborators possess an inadequate understanding of the rationale and intent underlying the particular strategic approach they've been conscripted to support. Unfortunately, to this day, specialists and their supporters are likely to neglect or downplay their project's inherent need for the kind of broad-based body of knowledge that team members are able to fall back on when they need to identify the task at hand: determining the when, where, by whom, and more importantly, Why.

In summary, the process of building and subsequently managing a multi-disciplinary and cross-functional capabilities (especially during the early stages of collaborative planning) represents a new level of operational capability for project teams responsible for the success of high-risk initiatives. Building such capabilities represents an even greater challenge when the organization's success depends on the performance of team members and stakeholders distributed across numerous departmental or geographical locations.

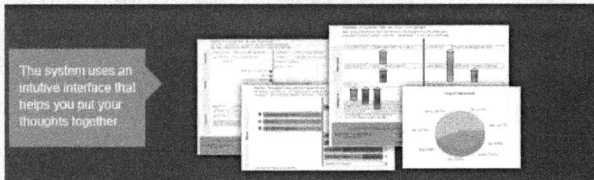

TEAM MEMBER RESPONSES

The system uses an intuitive interface that helps you put your thoughts together

When project teams are spread across great distances (and perhaps time-zones), the need to keep the entire group workflow proceeding smoothly can present a major challenge to team members, project managers and sponsors alike. But when long-distance collaborators are afforded the advantages of an electronic workspace, the very nature of these systems ordinarily provides the means to avoid major slowdowns or miscommunications.

As for the U-Template, its shared workspace provides a well-integrated communications system and a well-coordinated task schedule (collectively developing untried but promising ideas by fitting them jigsaw-like into a big picture), a step-by-step process that eventually doubles as the project end-product itself. As the screenshots above reveal, the U-Template mechanism also tracks and tabulates all collaborator contributions to the project, now fully arrayed on the screen as overviews of both individual and group responses to the Big Idea.

But the ability to collaborate easily under these conditions will ultimately maintain the integrity of the project's timing, budget, resources, and stakeholder expectations. Finally, as mentioned, projects ideally require data-recovery mechanisms that encourage individuals to contribute to, and tap into, the organization's "knowledge archive". Unfortunately, these tools are often non-existent.

With these imperatives in mind, many organizations employing traditional (often highly quantitative) risk models are looking for simpler and more user-friendly planning tools and methodologies. In the recent past they have become more and more aware of the fact that unwieldy approaches to managing complex matters are rendered even more so by overly sophisticated instruments. In contrast to such tools and methods, the U-Template affords project teams the much-needed conceptual and practical simplicity when it comes time for gathering and leveraging collaborator input, as well as a more efficient and effective mechanism for conducting thorough stakeholder analyses.[1]

However, developing both high-fidelity and broadband approaches to project planning requires the kind of conceptualization that may be relatively new to most organizations. As a rule of thumb, the larger the project scope and time frame, the higher the uncertainties, especially when a risk element is embedded in the context of another such contingency, and/or when a subsidiary objective is likely to combine with other project targets and goals. Therefore, collaborative teams must be equipped with tools designed to manage risk at the highest level of complexity and in doing so, support high-end executive decision-making when it comes to giving or not giving risky projects the green light.

The U-Template, has been developed in response to the need to deal with interwoven project contingencies within a systems-thinking perspective, providing a frame of reference wide enough to capture most—if not all—of the interdependencies that might exist within highly complex projects.[2]

1. There's another reason for the need of simpler analytic approaches: collaborators, especially project managers, often fail to fully understand their projects holistically. Research performed by data-provider Dun and Bradstreet on project success rates highlights the need for improved project definition with particular emphasis on scope, work breakdown, resource requirements, risk factors, and timing. Examples of major project failures at companies such as Coca Cola, AOL, and Starbucks all point towards methods and tools that failed to provide the big-picture perspective that might reveal hazardous large-scale systemic interdependencies.
2. It should be noted that when a systems thinking approach is employed by a

Every U-Template procedure and output, together with all team-member inputs, can be stored in an organization database as a reminder of past pre-project decisions or, for reasons of personnel assessment, how often and how effectively each team member has contributed creative input.

All told, the U-Template:

- Provides an electronic collaboration tool regardless of where its users may be located, departmentally or geographically, within or outside the organization. It lends collaborators the ability to view a common set of issues as viewed through the varied perceptual lenses that exist throughout the organization.

- Provides collaborators with a common frame of reference and comprehensible units of analysis.

- Allows user-participants to keep "all things considered at all times".

- Helps codify the organization's tacit (unspoken or undocumented) knowledge.

- Ensures that group discourse is less likely to get mired down in irrelevant, issues, biases or collective group-think.

Finally, the U-Template is a natural sales tool. (In a sense, the U-Template *is* the sales meeting.) Once a marketing representative has had a preliminary meeting with a

project team chartered with responsibility for a high risk initiative, its chances of success improve dramatically. An abundance of published data supports the practical utility of this type of systems thinking. For example, a project team at Massachusetts General Hospital, one of the best health facilities in the world, succeeded in reducing patient throughput time by 75% when using this approach.

potential client or buyer and then takes the time to U-Template a business proposition, he or she can return to the customer and deliver a full presentation assisted by a highly organized and coherent visual display.

ABOUT THE AUTHOR

David Herman is the creator of a number of software products, among them the U-Template for business planning and BlunderBuster for planning major life-changes. In addition to his decades-long clinical work in paradigmatic psychoanalysis, the author, a former New Yorker now residing in New Zealand, is an award-winning research psychologist and has published articles on mental imagery in both the *Psychoanalytic Review* (where he was on the editorial board) and the *American Imago*. He has also organized and presented programs on scientific, cultural and political matters for the Association for Applied Psychoanalysis at the New York Academy of Science.

Contact the author at davidherman@vodafone.co.nz

www.u-template.com

www.ingramcontent.com/pod-product-compliance
Lightning Source LLC
Chambersburg PA
CBHW070729220326
41598CB00024BA/3369